Changing Faces of Adult Literacy, Language and Numeracy

a critical history

Changing Faces of Adult Literacy, Language and Numeracy

a critical history

Mary Hamilton and Yvonne Hillier

Trentham Books

Stoke on trent, UK and Sterling, USA

Trentham Books Limited

Westview House	22883 Quicksilver Drive
734 London Road	Sterling
Oakhill	VA 20166-2012
Stoke on Trent	USA
Staffordshire	
England ST4 5NP	

© 2006 Mary Hamilton and Yvonne Hillier

First published 2006

British Library Cataloguing-in-Publication Data
A catalogue record for this book is available from the British Library

ISBN-13: 978-1-85856-348-0
ISBN-10: 1-85856-348-8

Designed and typeset by Trentham Print Design Ltd, Chester and printed in Great Britain by Cromwell Press Ltd, Trowbridge.

Contents

For Jacob and Alice

and

*For the members of the Research and Practice in
Adult Literacy Network, past, present and future*

Acknowledgements

We ourselves have lived through the history we present here. Along the way we have been inspired by many people. Many more have contributed generously to the project we report here and we owe them all an enormous debt.

First, those who volunteered their time to be interviewed, sometimes travelling across the country or writing lengthy e-mails to us, editing and adding commentaries and finding materials to donate to the archive.

Second, those who carried out the interviews and spent many hours documenting them and editing transcripts: Yvon Appleby, Gill O'Toole, Candice Satchwell, Iffat Shahnaz and Barbara Walker. Thirdly, the transcribers: Irene Smith, Gaye Olde, Maggie Lackey, Cheryl Scott and Alice Jesmont.

We worked closely with Sam Parsons who helped us select the National Child Development Survey sample, carried out some of the interviews and met us regularly to develop and discuss the project.

Our advisory group offered guidance throughout, reading materials, making suggestions and keeping us going through their belief in the importance of the project. They were Helen Casey, Noyona Chanda, Jay Derrick, John Field, Sue Grief, Margaret Herrington, Ann Hodgson, Peter Lavender, Jane Mace, Jenny Ozga and Jane Ward.

We are particularly indebted to two people who shared their extensive knowledge with us and who are both in the process of writing related books: Sheila Rosenberg on ESOL and Peter Clyne on the impact of the 1973 Russell Report on Adult Education. Additional specialist research assistance was given by Tamsin Heycock, Kathy Pitt, David Renton and Patricia Worgan. We had useful conversations with David James and Juliet Merrifield. David Barton, Fiona Frank, Oliver Fulton, Wendy Moss and John Pratt read drafts of our writing. Tom Hamilton checked references and helped design the timelines.

Thanks also to those who gave administrative help, organising databases, setting up the website and the archive, designing publicity and supporting the research team and advisory group: Jon Blanchard, Sue Burrows, Helen Clish, Dee Daglish, Lyn Drake, Steve Jenkins, Jas Kaur, Nick Pearce, Lauren Proctor, Alison Sharman, Karen Small and Richard Stone.

Our work was supported by a grant from the ESRC (R000239387) between January 2002 and June 2004 to the University of Lancaster, City University and the Institute of Education, London University. The National Research and Development Centre (NRDC) provided additional funds for the archiving of documents.

The opinions and interpretations we express in this book are, of course, our own responsibility and are intended to be a springboard for further debate and research.

Mary Hamilton, Yvonne Hillier, December 2005

Introduction

This book follows the development of adult literacy, numeracy and English for Speakers of Other Languages (ESOL) from the early 1970s *Right To Read* campaign, to 2000 when they became a central focus of national government policy in England through the *Skills for Life* strategy (SK4L). It follows ESOL from its separate origins in the early Neighbourhood English and other home tuition schemes for Asian women in the 1960s to becoming an integrated (though still contested) part of basic skills provision.

The story we have to tell is of the invention of a new field of educational practice, of how it has moved from the margins of educational policy into the mainstream, gradually gaining in status across the period we have studied. We show how it has moved from the fragmentary opportunities originally offered to adults, underpinned by voluntary tutors and organisations, to a more standardised and formal service, a process that has accelerated rapidly under the *Skills for Life* strategy since 2000. We try to give a sense of how this process was experienced by those most closely involved as learners, practitioners and policy actors; document how tensions and dilemmas have been managed; what has been gained and what has been lost along the way.

This is the story of how an initially unorganised domain of social action has struggled to be seen as a legitimate area of educational activity, whilst having to engage with deep shifts in national policy priorities that redefined the funding sources, goals and discourse of the emerging field. Part of this story is about the integration of new activities and new learners into existing institutions and how this has set up tensions and possibilities for change within those organisations.

Three linked strands

An important part of the story is how three quite distinct areas, ESOL, numeracy and literacy, have been welded together under the umbrella term 'adult basic skills'. In this amalgam, literacy has always been seen as the most powerful partner. Numeracy, despite its high importance for everyday opportunities in employment and education, has been a much less visible and resourced field (see Coben, 2006). ESOL, with its strong links to English as a Foreign Language (EFL), to the politics of immigration and language policy, to debates around language variety, racism and international developments, has been yoked uneasily with basic skills. The link owes more to our perceptions of immigrant groups and the relationship between English and the other languages of the UK than it does to fundamental similarities of ESOL with adult numeracy and literacy. Ignoring the diverse origins of immigrant groups, it makes the erroneous assumption that those who cannot speak English are uneducated (Schellekens, 2001). While this makes it a fascinating and essential part of the story of how the field of adult basic skills has developed, there is a longer and richer history of ESOL to be written in its own right.

The field we are describing in this book has been referred to in many different ways since the 1970s and its changing names signal important instabilities and debates. In this book we refer to Adult Language, Literacy and Numeracy (ALLN) throughout, which is an acronym that readers in 2005 will recognise, even as it is being superseded by other terms.

In some respects ALLN is a unique story with its own cast of extraordinary actors, colourful and varied settings, crises and myths, triumphs and a set of what Levin and others have called 'wicked' issues that surface time and again (Levin, 2005; Rittel and Webber, 1973). In other respects, its struggles will be recognised by others working in any newly developing field of social policy. For example, the need to raise awareness through innovative and high-profile publicity campaigns, the search for ways of presenting the issues to catch public interest and funding whilst creating positive representations of those seen to be in need; the movement from voluntary pressure groups to secure government funding are aspects that will be recognised by campaigners in many other new areas of education and social policy. The struggle for legitimation has involved raising the status of ALLN as a fundable area within social policy. establishing its credibility within practice and professional development, and, within the academy, as a valid area for research.

Also recognisable will be the twists and turns in the fortunes of this new field as the policy and political climate around it changes, sometimes supporting it and sometimes brutally ignoring it. As a marginal and fragmented field operating in a complex social environment, ALLN has been disproportionately affected by forces not designed with its own priorities in mind. As one practitioner said of a bruising experience of re-structuring an adult community learning service:

> I never felt it was directed at me ... or that it was directed at basic skills. I felt the basic skills and ESOL went down by accident because they were getting rid of the rest ... it was a mistake, definitely, I know that. (RP, Manchester)

Practitioners and policy actors alike have had to weather such storms and hook into other social projects and sources of funding. A recurrent metaphor is that of 'working in the cracks' as a description of how it feels to try to sustain and develop ALLN through changing funding and policy regimes.

Our story

When we met at a conference in July 1998, we were about to find out what a committee, chaired by Sir Claus Moser, was going to say about the state of basic skills provision in England. The report of this committee (Moser, 1999) led to the *Skills for Life* strategy in England. Change was in the air and we realised that we were in danger of losing the practices of the past in the rush to a future that would have little institutional memory. As people in the field retired, their stories and experiences would leave with them. We decided to apply for research funds to help us capture the history, and examine it to help us deal with the future implementation of whatever policy was going to arise from Moser's report.

We had both become involved with adult literacy as volunteers in the 1970s. Yvonne began to teach literacy and numeracy on a part-time basis, and subsequently became an organiser in two Outer London boroughs before moving out of direct basic skills work into training teachers in adult and further education. Finally she moved into higher education where she began to further her research following her doctorate on good practice in adult basic education. By now, in the late 1990s, she was keenly aware of the national and international perspectives on adult basic education, but continued to be influenced by her own experiences as a volunteer, part time tutor and organiser, to the extent that the practitioners' story is uppermost in her research interests. Mary began as a volunteer for the Elfrida Rathbone Society in Islington and became a part-time tutor in the East London adult education service. She continued to teach adults in the US during the later 1970s while she finished a PhD on children's communication skills and returned to a research post at Lancaster University in 1981. By then, she had become aware of a gap between the worlds of research and practice that she has worked ever since to close, helping to establish ALLN as a credible field of academic research and working with practitioners via professional development programmes, collaborative research projects and the Research and Practice in Adult Literacy group (*RaPAL*).

Defining the research

We had to place boundaries around our research and in the end we concentrated only on England, although the policies we are describing also applied to Wales for much of the time period we studied. The histories of Scotland and Northern Ireland have woven in and out of English policy. We refer to these at specific points but make no claim to offer a comprehensive picture. Each of the countries of the UK has its own complexity and context and each deserves its own account. The divergence between them has accelerated with devolution, as described in Crowther *et al*, 2001. We also briefly cover the wider international context as it has impinged on the UK and we indicate sources for further information about policies in other countries.

We focus on a 30-year period from 1970-2000 as the period within which ALLN assumed status as a field and became a social policy focus. There is a much longer and wider view that others have already explored in much more detail. We can only signal interested readers towards this literature that describes earlier initiatives for adult literacy (Jones and Marriott, 1995); periodic moral panics about literacy standards (Rogers, 1984; Soler and Openshaw, 2005); the moral and political economies of reading and writing (Brandt, 2005; Graff, 1987; Williams, 1965); the social history of the communication media (Briggs and Burke, 2005) and of literacy especially (Vincent, 2000; Stephens, 1990; Mace, 2002; Howard, 1991); the long struggle for universal access to education and specific curriculum initiatives in education (Simon, 1993).

Our research focused on three groups of storytellers: policy actors, practitioners and learners. All three groups took part in interviews to help us build a bigger story and for this book we have read and drawn extensively on the many hours of taped interviews that people patiently gave and edited with us. It has been a hard process to summarise and we are aware of how little of our detailed data it has been possible to include here. The quotes we have used throughout the book have been carefully chosen because they are typical of many others and because they signal recurrent themes and disputes that people were concerned with. It is important to read this book as a first attempt to offer an overall shape to our many, rich and detailed findings and we are writing elsewhere about particular topics in more depth. (Shahnaz and Hamilton, 2005; Appleby and Hamilton, 2005; Hamilton, 2005; Hillier and Hamilton (2005). We are continuing to develop our website as a resource for the field http://www.literacy. lancaster.ac.uk/links/changingfaces.htm

The project also uncovered a mass of written documentation from all over the country. Interviewees donated teaching and training materials, local policy documents and examples of student writing. Many people had already written up something about their experiences in newsletters, project reports, local newspapers, dissertations and assignments on professional development courses. This 'grey literature' as it is often known, abounds in a field like ALLN and awaits future historians. Whilst we are committed to writing about our own interpretations and analysis, we see the archives we have assembled from this material as an equally important legacy of the Changing Faces project.

How to read this book

We have tried to make this book accessible to anyone currently working in ALLN who has a curiosity about how the field has developed and who questions why it is organised as it is. We expect it to be read quizzically by the many people who have played a part in these developments over the years, a large number of whom have contributed to the account we present here. We expect they will challenge and elaborate on the version of history we present. Specifically we think there are four things the reader can take from this book.

1. A better understanding of why current policy and practice in ALLN is organised as it is and how it has come to be that way; seeing ALLN as part of a bigger picture.
2. A sense that many of the issues we grapple with in the field are not temporary or inexplicable peculiarities of a misguided policy process, or the fault of individual personalities or of one organisation. They are more enduring tensions that have to be managed.
3. A better sense of where agency lies in the field, of what roles we might play in shaping it, wherever we are positioned; where it is worth applying pressure by putting in effort and where it is not.
4. Ideas and documentary sources which can be used in professional development courses and to carry out further research.
5. Resources that can be used in learning groups to enable adult learners to compare their experiences and views about learning, curriculum and teaching materials.

You can read Chapter 1 for a brief overview of the historical period. In Chapter 2 you can find out how we collected the data on which the history is based. Chapter 3 sets out the policy analysis framework that guides the structure of the subsequent chapters. Chapters 4, 5 and 6 give more detail to the historical overview from the perspectives of adult learners, practitioners and policy actors. Chapters 7 to 10 develop specific themes: the changing nature of provision, methods and curriculum; assessment and finally, strategies for publicity and recruitment. Chapter 11 offers our conclusions, summarising what we have learned about change and agency and the spaces we have identified for public debate under different policy regimes. It is quite possible to dip into the parts of the book that interest you most, but we would recommend reading Chapter 1 first, unless you are already familiar with the broad outline of developments since the 1970s.

Our exploration of history and our comparisons with other national contexts (see Lo Bianco and Wickert, 2001; McKenna, 2005) have taught us that, however far the field has come, the search for a better world of literacy is not a straightforward evolution. *Skills for Life* will not last for ever and we can expect continuing changes and set backs. The problem of sustaining adequate learning opportunities for ALLN is entangled in a broader field of forces which are explored in this book.

PART ONE

1

A sense of history

There are at least two million functionally illiterate adults in England and Wales. They are either unable to read or write, or they have a reading age of less than that you would expect in a nine year. (*Right to Read* Manifesto p.22)

None of us had a clue about how to run a campaign; we didn't even know that we really were running a campaign to begin with, although we did eventually realise it ... I don't think any of us quite realised what it did for this country. For us it was a seminal thing – a tipping point. (JS, BBC Development Officer)

In 1975, a series of BBC programmes entitled *On the Move* were broadcast on prime time Sunday evening television. Using a combination of celebrity characters, a humorous 'sit-com' format and personal testimonies from adult learners, the innovative ten minute programmes were aimed at adults who needed to improve their literacy. They also raised public awareness of the fact that, despite the system of compulsory secondary schooling that had existed for thirty years, adults could still have problems with reading, writing and spelling. For the first time, the programmes were linked to a telephone helpline encouraging adults to come forward for help with literacy and, by the end of 1978, up to three hundred calls per week were being received. Many people (90% of them women) also called to volunteer themselves as tutors for those who needed help (Hargreaves, 1980).

The BBC's decision to create the programmes came about as a result of a single issue campaign by community-based activists in a voluntary organisation, The British Association of Settlements (BAS). The BAS claimed, on the basis of surveys of literacy among school leavers, that around 2 million adults were in need of help. The aim of the campaign was to persuade both central government and local authorities to support the development of a new area of educational practice (BAS, 1973).

A commitment to fund this new area of educational practice was sought not only within the local authorities, but also nationally through parliament. The MP Chris Price asked a private member's question about 'illiterate' adults leading to the decision in 1975 by Gerry Fowler, then Minister of State for Education, to identify one million pounds to set up an Adult Literacy Resource Agency (ALRA). The money was obtained from an underspend in the university library budget and would support the local education authorities (LEAs) as they began responding to the demand for literacy teaching (Fowler, 1988; Withnall, 1994). Over the next thirty years, literacy classes for adults grew in number. The form of provision changed from primarily one-to-one teaching by volunteers, to small group teaching, supplemented by drop-in centres and e-learning. Teaching took place in adult and community learning centres, prisons, further education colleges, employment training centres, workplaces, in voluntary organisations, and in people's own homes.

Following a review of adult basic skills by Sir Claus Moser in 1999 (The Moser Report), the government in England funded a *Skills for Life* strategy, setting ambitious targets for improvement (DfES, 2001). It created a specialised qualification structure for adult basic skills and a set of professional standards to which practitioners must adhere. Core curricula in ESOL, numeracy and literacy have aligned adult programmes with performance in school-based subjects. In 2004 the strategy met its aim of 750,000 adults gaining an appropriate qualification. Further targets have now been set so that by 2010, a total of 2.25 million adults will have improved their basic skills.

Inventing a new educational space

When the BBC programmes and the adult literacy campaign burst on to the scene in 1975, adult literacy did not exist as a recognised field of educational practice. There were sporadic programmes: in the army, in prisons, on day-release courses at technical colleges, and in voluntary schemes; the provision had a variety of names, including 'General Studies' or 'Remedial English' (Jones and Marriott, 1995).

The Army has always drawn large numbers of young men who were in the past, according to army jargon, 'accidental illiterates' (White, 1963, p74). During the Second World War, large numbers were exposed as having lower levels of literacy and numeracy. After the war, young men doing their National

Service continued to need basic education to help them meet the army's minimum requirement of 'working literacy' (White, 1963, p185). The Preliminary Education Centres developed teaching and learning techniques contextualised within the Army setting. Readers and worksheets were created with examples of Army functions involving literacy and numeracy skills. By the time that the adult literacy campaign took place in 1973, the Army had a well-established programme of basic education in place. Many prisons and borstals also offered basic literacy tuition (Bayliss, 2003). However, despite offers to share their practice, with the exception of the prison service and one or two London boroughs, the Army's development of basic education went largely unnoticed.

Outside prison and the armed forces, there was no obvious place in the UK for an older person to go for help with literacy. Some found their way to programmes organised by social welfare projects and local authority adult education (Clyne, 1972; Devereux, 1982; Haviland, 1973). For adults who had left or had been dismissed from school at the earliest opportunity, an 'O' level English Literature or maths class was not a suitable place to learn the basics of literacy or numeracy. People arriving as immigrants who needed to learn or improve their English language, had some provision, started before 1970, but this was within the background of a generally patchy and ill-funded system of adult education. Not much is recorded about what the learners did or how they felt about what was on offer at the time.

A field that is emerging has no fixed name or form. It is an imaginary space, figured in some people's minds, and takes chaotic and fragmentary form at first, shifting shape to fit whatever kind of organisation and physical place will host it. This state of emergence, of half-reality, is reflected strongly in our data to an extent that surprised us when we first began to gather in the record and the stories. The route into the field for the tutors was as chaotic and patchy as that of the learners. People, mostly women, told stories of their haphazard and accidental entry into the field, falling into jobs that would be the start of a lifelong fascination and career for many of them. For example: 'I applied for six jobs, five in schools and one in a further education college. The college interviewed me first and I took the job'; 'My sister-in-law persuaded me'; 'My husband worked for the LEA and they needed a tutor'; 'I saw a notice in the college where I was a student'. They scanned opportunistically for part-time job vacancies to fit in with their complicated lives as young mothers, or as people moving from one area to another, or searching for a different career. The work looked interesting and worthwhile and no experience or qualifications were necessary.

The fragmentation in the field in the 1970s can also be traced through both the different institutional spaces and the physical environments available for learning and teaching. Practitioners' jobs were not standardised. They had a range of names, including 'Remedial English' 'Compensatory Classes', 'General Studies' 'Learning Support', 'Adult Literacy' and later 'Fresh Start' and 'Second Chance to Learn'. They might be employed by a department of English or engineering, or managed and organised in different ways in the prospectuses of adult education centres, colleges and community groups.

A glance at the physical places where teaching and learning took place illustrates the journey vividly, showing textures of the imagined space of ALLN. There were no dedicated or purpose-built rooms for the work to be carried out and practitioners are full of exasperated accounts of work in makeshift, ill-equipped, disrepaired and inappropriate venues: portacabins, huts at the back of the car park, disused attic rooms up inaccessible stairways, and old warehouses, primary school classrooms with tiny chairs, prison rooms with 'horrible green tables'. Sometimes people landed in a comfortable room, but available spaces were frequently temporary and classes had to move on before long. The nomadic life of the part-time tutor is part of the mythology of the field; 'we were always being moved about from one building to another'.

This, then, is very much the story of how new institutional and physical spaces for learning were created to make room for ALLN. For those working and learning at the start it was an imagined space and has remained so for much of the time until the 1990s, when legislation put a definite shape around it and located it firmly as a designated subject area within further education (FE). At a stroke, this fixed the boundaries of what could be called ALLN and inevitably left some activities and some people outside the formal, business-oriented space of FE. The solidifying of the field in this way left alternative visions unacknowledged (see Hamilton, 1997).

Nothing comes from nothing: roots in the 1960s and earlier
The emerging field of ALLN did not start entirely from scratch. Since 1948, UNESCO had promoted adult literacy in developing countries without formal schooling systems whilst Western European countries returned statistics recording a zero for illiteracy. There were recent precedents in the international mass literacy campaigns in countries such as Cuba and the Soviet Union and the US *Right to Read* campaign. In Italy, the *150 hours* programme had addressed basic education in the workplace (Mace and Yarnit, 1987). The

radical literacy work of the Brazilian educator, Paulo Freire, was published for the first time in English (Freire, 1972).

It is hard now to bring back the feeling of the time, but for many people interested in social justice, alternative realities seemed possible at the beginning of the 1970s. Turning something you could only glimpse into hard, everyday, established, practice seemed entirely feasible and, indeed, many of the social movements and organisations that we now take for granted, including the housing charity, Shelter, the Child Poverty Action Group, women's aid and consumer advice agencies were started at that time (see Curtis and Sanderson, 2004). This spirit of the time carried many of those who worked in adult literacy, numeracy and ESOL at the beginning. Though many tutors did not have directly political motivations, the women's movement, civil rights for ethnic minority groups, class and feminist politics and a strong trade union movement provided a backdrop to their activities. This was particularly evident in community development focused programmes that had a broad agenda of widening access to education and as part of a social justice strategy, for example the 'Second Chance to Learn' course in Liverpool (see Yarnitt in Thompson 1980). Such programmes have continued throughout the period we have studied. They are part of an access movement with its own history that intersects importantly with adult literacy, language and numeracy (Davies, 2000).

An influential minority of those practitioners who entered the field did so because they saw it as an opportunity to engage with a radical cultural politics centred on access to education, class privilege and language, a cultural politics that was articulated in relation to schooling by such writers as Harold Rosen, Chris Searle, Herbert Kohl and Basil Bernstein (see O'Rourke, 2005). The work of these writers had wide currency and was included in teacher training courses at the time. Ideas about de-schooling, and growing interests in popular culture and oral history were also influential (Morley and Worpole, 1982). Ivan Illich, an advocate for the de-schooling movement, was referred to approvingly by the minister responsible for releasing the original funding for adult literacy, Gerry Fowler (Fowler, 1988). These ideas, and especially the notion that literacy should be linked to community development and anti-poverty initiatives, was institutionally reinforced in certain LEAs (such as the Inner London Education Authority and Leicestershire) and in Scotland where ALLN developed very differently as a result (see Crowther *et al*, 2001). At first, Scotland was included in the remit of the new resource agency, but after this a separate agency, the Scottish Adult Literacy Agency (SCALA) was set up. This agency became absorbed into community education provision which some have argued resulted in a loss of identity for basic skills work

English provision for speakers of other languages, ESOL, has enjoyed a longer history than that of literacy or numeracy and has from the start been part of government attempts to control and manage immigrants who arrived from the new commonwealth countries and elsewhere. The 1962 Commonwealth Immigration Act introduced the first measures to control immigration from the Commonwealth. This was followed in 1963 by a Ministry of Education Pamphlet 43 *English for Immigrants* identifying the challenge facing teachers in schools and affirming the need for adults to learn English.

Funding for ESOL teaching was provided for the first time in 1967 under Section 11 of the Local Government Act of 1966. In part this was a response to Enoch Powell's 'rivers of blood' speech where he argued that too much immigration would lead to confrontation. Local authorities could claim 50 per cent of their costs (later 75%) retrospectively from the central government Home Office. The early policy, reflected in the model of funding, was integrationist and illustrates how closely ESOL has been linked to the politics of race and immigration throughout this period (See Carby, 1982). ESOL materials were developed for use in schools and also used with adult students and on teacher training courses (Schools Council, 1967).

While increasing provision was being made for children in schools, some attention was also paid to workers who did not have English as their first language. The Industrial Training Act 1966 allowed for training to be set up, but by 1969 little had been done to take advantage of this funding. Birmingham LEA established classes on employers' premises and the London Borough of Ealing set up the Pathway Centre in conjunction with the Careers Service in 1968 to provide courses for newly arrived, non-English speaking teenagers to prepare them to move on to work. Both LEAs used Section 11 money for these initiatives.

These strands represent the backdrop to the field that subsequently emerged, affecting its shape and some of the tensions that it has had to struggle with ever since. They have affected the resources made available to the newly developing field. They dealt with the organisation of provision, as well as determining the available discourses and limiting assumptions and prejudices. As we will see below, over time these strands have been overlaid by broader and growing policy influences. In particular, the role of vocational training and the agencies responsible for it became increasingly important.

Shaping factors

The period between the early 1970s and 2000 was a time characterised by radical shifts in the landscape of public policy (see Chitty, 1989, 2004; Gleeson and Shane, 1999; Jones, 2003; Lawson and Silver, 1973 for overviews). Education was a particularly sharply fought battleground and ALLN bears all the scars of these battles, travelling as it has from 'old' to 'new' capitalist times (see Gee *et al*, 1996).

After the expansionist period of the 1960s, the 1970s saw a growing realisation that compulsory schooling as developed since the war had not achieved a basic education for everyone as hoped. The National Foundation for Educational Research (NFER) carried out research which suggested that, after a steady upward trend, improvements in standards of literacy and numeracy had slowed down during the 1960s (Start and Wells, 1972).

The notion of compensatory education was at its height. This was the moment of the Halsey report into Educational Priority Areas (1972) and the era of Community Development Projects as a radical intervention intended to solve well-recognised but intractable problems of social inequality. There was a general concern about increasing access to higher education for working class and other disadvantaged groups, of which the establishment of the Open University in 1971 was a part. This concern was strongly expressed in the Russell Report which recommended that 'LEAs should make available and widely known opportunities for men and women to complete formal general education' (DES, 1973, para 183) though this was still seen in terms of 'remedial' education rather than a part of lifelong learning.

The early 1970s mark the end of the post-war settlement in education and social policy (see Finch, 1984), a time of widespread progressive social change and civil rights movements, and also the period when the UK finally joined the European Community. The International Monetary Fund (IMF) crisis of 1976 occurred just as the adult literacy campaign was gathering momentum. Unemployment was beginning to rise. Progressive approaches to education had long been under attack by the cultural restorationists who desired to restore traditional English cultural values and to maintain a coherent and narrow view of national identity (see Cox and Dyson, 1969). Educational policy was taking a decisive turn towards a modernistic vocationalism under the Labour government of Callaghan (signalled by Callaghan's Ruskin speech in 1976. See Chitty, 2004).

So by the time Margaret Thatcher's conservative government was elected in 1979 the trend towards vocationalism was already strong. It accelerated under the Conservative administrations of the 1980s and 1990s (Wolf, 2002; Hyland and Merrill, 2003; and Lumby and Foskett, 2005). The Conservatives ruthlessly restructured the public services and their attendant discourses and the education system was marketised. Unemployment was allowed to rise and was a central issue during the 1980s and early 1990s. As Jones (2003) and others have noted, these tendencies did not always result in coherent policies, but produced conflicting pressures on the educational system: for example the dilemma of how to deal with diversity and choice whilst working with strong centralised control.

Funding has had a profound influence upon provision. From Home Office funding for ESOL and prison education through to the multi-million funding for *Skills for Life* after 2000, the field has taken shape as a result of the differing funding sources which practitioners and managers were able to draw upon. The effects of funding decisions and the mechanisms put in place for accountability and control of public spending, interweave through all our respondents' stories and throughout the chapters in this book.

Four key policy phases
We have identified four phases to describe the last three decades of policy and practice. Each phase is characterised by *shifting power between the different agencies* involved, *changes in the public discourses* that define ALLN and different degrees of visibility for the three main specialist areas of numeracy, ESOL and literacy. There are connections between the developments in the field described to us by the people we interviewed and broader political and cultural changes, both national and international. Key moments marking the vocationalisation and marketisation of education are vividly recalled by our informants.

Phase 1 Mid 1970s: A Literacy Campaign is led by a coalition of voluntary agencies with a powerful media partner, the BBC
Advocacy by individual members of the government successfully exploited an interest in adult education for disadvantaged adults, opened up by the publication of the Russell Report in 1973. One million pounds was released to set up a national resource agency and to increase LEA provision (Fowler, 1988; Withnall, 1994). LEAs and the adult education establishment were enrolled in the campaign along with thousands of volunteer tutors and adult learners who began to work in one-to-one home tuition, or in small groups with paid part-time teachers. By 1976, 15,000 adults were receiving literacy tuition across England and Wales.

The agency was based in London and employed regional development officers who travelled widely within their patch. Practitioners around the country used the free newsletter, materials and guides to teaching that the agency produced. It offered additional funding spread across the country for Special Development Projects, and its regional training programme helped networks develop.

Before the campaign in 1972, a survey of local authority provision showed that just 5,000 adults were receiving help with reading and writing in England and Wales (Haviland, 1973). There were very important links between the British Association of Settlements (BAS) and the BBC who publicised the issue and pushed for the development of local responses. The BBC used its status and networks to lobby for the release of the initial funding. The Russell Report on Adult Education had just been published and, although its proposals were not implemented, it opened a policy space with its concern for 'disadvantaged adults' which the literacy campaign could fill. The social climate of the time was crucial. Some of the BAS campaigners were veterans of other contemporary social justice campaigns such as the housing campaign, Shelter, and brought in tactics they had learned from that experience.

It is important also to understand the BBC's public broadcasting mission that provided resources to committed individuals to carry out this project. In contrast, most LEAs and the adult education establishment of this period are represented as reluctant or unaware partners being dragged along with the campaign, although their provision for adult literacy had been slowly increasing across the 1960s (Haviland, 1973).

For ESOL, community-based local language schemes were vital in providing English tuition for adults, mainly women at home, who fell outside the provision being made in schools and the nascent courses for people in work. A survey of Asian women over the age of 44 at the time, found that 82 per cent of those interviewed were judged to have little or no English (Smith, 1977:56). Neighbourhood English classes were established across a number of north London boroughs, pioneered by Ruth Hayman in 1969. Similar schemes rapidly developed across the country. This year also saw major initiatives led by two of the major players in the development of ESOL: the BBC piloted and broadcast a series of programmes called *Parosi*, and the Commission for Racial Equality (CRE) published the *Home Tutor Kit*. In 1974 ESOL support was offered in workplaces for the first time through the National Centre for Industrial Language Training, funded with European money through the Manpower Services Commission (MSC).

The Manpower Services Commission (MSC) was formed in 1973 before the literacy campaign started. As well as the Industrial Language Training programme, it was already running full-time Training Opportunities Programme (TOPS) courses within which people could improve their basic literacy and numeracy skills (see Ainley and Corney,1990; Field, 1996). The MSC was to become increasingly influential as time went on.

During this period there were some very clear actors and drivers of change, notably the media and campaigning pressure groups. The initiative was carried forward by volunteers recruited through the media campaign, and LEA responses were very varied (see ALRA reports, 1976, 1977). Some offered strong support to the new field, including the Inner London Education Authority (ILEA) which set up a Language and Literacy Unit (LLU) This galvanised efforts in London and was to become very influential throughout the period we have studied, although it encountered difficulties and pressures that mirror the fate of the field more generally. At the end of this phase, the Advisory Council for Adult and Continuing Education reviewed adult literacy (ACACE, 1979) concluding that ALLN could longer be seen as a temporary problem to be solved through a one-off campaign. ACACE proposed the establishment of a permanent service and national agency.

Phase 2 1980s: Provision developed substantially, supported by Local Education Authority Adult Education Services and voluntary organisations, with leadership, training and development funding from a national agency

In 1980, adult literacy was expanded to include numeracy and became known as Adult Basic Education (ABE). In 1984, ESOL was added to the remit of the national agency, now known as The Adult Literacy and Basic Skills Unit (ALBSU) and an uneasy relationship developed. By 1985, ALBSU estimated 110,000 adults received tuition and programmes were drawing on substantial additional funding from the MSC and the European Social Fund (ESF).

Funding for the national agency was reviewed frequently by central government and, despite the recommendations from the ACACE report, no further national policy commitment was made. The agency was put in the position of having to constantly justify its existence and come up with innovative and dynamic ideas

Because of the lack of central direction, the extent and quality of provision was highly dependent on local authorities and the voluntary and pressure groups that lobbied them. County and metropolitan networks (including advisory staff) were central to practitioners during this period.

As statutory provision increased, ALBSU became a more confident national presence. In its various incarnations it was a major focus for ALLN and became the 'official voice' of the field in England and Wales, presenting a public image of the field both to government and the general public. It was crucial in providing coherence to these local developments and was uncontested on the national scene. It developed a programme of regional training events and made available Special Project funds (see Charnley and Withnall, 1985)

Because of its access to substantial funding from the European Union (EU), the Department of Employment (DoE), the MSC became increasingly influential and funded much basic literacy and numeracy through its programmes for the unemployed during the Thatcher years. Throughout the 1980s, the DoE encroached on areas that had previously been the remit of the Department for Education and Science (DES), causing competition and tension in the field (see Parkes, 1985).

Full-time Training Opportunities Scheme (TOPS) courses continued to be funded until 1986 and their demise was bitterly resisted by some managers and organisers. Access courses flourished and voluntary bodies such as the Workers Educational Association (WEA) developed courses for women returning to study (Hutchinson, 1980).

The voluntary organisations continued to innovate but their work was less nationally visible and increasingly marginalised. Many schemes such as the National Federation of Voluntary Literacy Schemes experimented with student writing and publishing activities and these were initially supported by ALBSU (see Gardener, undated; Frost and Hoy, 1980). A number of community publishing projects flourished, such as Gatehouse Books, Centerprise and The Book Place in London, the *Write First Time* newspaper collective. For a short while, a National Students Association (NSA) was formed. Research and practice networks, and experiments in learning democracy such as the Lee Centre, Goldsmiths College and Pecket Well College were all expressions of a vision to do things differently *with* (rather than *for*) adult learners.

The role of the media changed. The BBC no longer led autonomous public awareness campaigns but continued to create programmes subject to the advice or request of the national agency. These were more closely and narrowly targeted and subject to policy priorities (see Chapter 10).

The nature of the student body in ALLN also changed, partly reflecting economic changes and immigration patterns, with many more women, unemployed adults and those referred from other services. Numeracy was beginning to be a differentiated presence within adult basic education. But ALBSU was unable to progress the ESOL agenda nationally. It had little funding, vision or analysis of the links between language and literacy policy and the political climate was hostile to immigration and to minority language rights (see the Linguistic Minorities Project, 1985, report for context at the time; also ALBSU, 1989b).

The Conservative government was interested in basic skills insofar as they were relevant to solving the problem of the steadily growing numbers of un-employed adults resulting from its economic policies. When it abolished ILEA in 1989 and reduced the funding and local democratic power of the LEAs, ALLN was, however, disproportionately affected (see Lobley and Moss, 1990). As a marginal area of provision within an adult education service itself under threat from cuts in LEA funding, it became very vulnerable and was un-noticed when reforms were proposed which threatened it.

But ALLN, too, changed. It changed through the energetic, strategic activity of ALBSU who used their limited resources to produce high quality pub-lications. ALBSU paid careful attention to public relations with the govern-ment, through editorials in its newsletters and by taking advantage of any opportunities for short term funding of new projects. ALLN also changed through the activities of practitioners on the ground, who innovated methods and materials, advocated for and protected resources for their students and their communities by whatever means they could. ALLN adapted to the changing institutional and funding context within which it was a fragmented and low status area of provision.

This was not a consultative policy regime. Teachers, like other professional and employee groups, were largely excluded from the social policy process as part of a wider government strategy to reduce trade union influence on public policy. Their part-time contracts and limited access to professional training meant that ALLN tutors were slow to develop a professional voice.

Phase 3 1989 to 1998: Reduction of LEA funding and control, statutory status of ALLN through a more formalised further education (FE) system, dependent on funding through a national funding body.

Although the 1988 Education Reform Act was arguably the most important piece of educational legislation during this period, it was the 1992 Further and Higher Education Act that most affected the future shape of ALLN. The colleges became incorporated businesses, responsible for their own financial affairs, and an era of competition arose between providers, as they were encouraged to increase student numbers, but with a reduction in the unit funding. The funding regime introduced with incorporation of colleges had radical effects on further and adult education more generally and ALLN within it. All further education courses were taken out of LEA control and funded by a new body, the Further Education Funding Council (FEFC) with its own inspectorate.

ALBSU seized the opportunity to lobby for basic skills to be included in what was known as the 'Schedule 2' list so that it would be eligible for funding within the array of vocational courses included in FE Colleges. ALLN was designated as 'Programme Area 10' comprising adult literacy, numeracy, Special Learning Difficulties and Disabilities (SLDD) and ESOL. With the exception of SLDD (see Tomlinson,1996), these areas were not systematically distinguished in inspection reports, though colleges often knew the balance of strengths and weaknesses across the various sections of their own organisations.

The statutory status of ALLN thus changed. It became a designated area of vocational study within further education, with a new scope and goals, and guaranteed free to all students. It was subject to a funding regime that stressed progression, vocational outcomes and qualifications and required formal audit. It was no longer primarily open-ended and community-focused. In 1995-6 ALBSU reported that 319,402 people were receiving tuition in England, two-thirds of whom were studying in the FE sector.

LEAs retained responsibility for non-vocational adult leisure courses, but with much reduced funding. Some metropolitan authorities, most notably ILEA, were abolished, leaving a decentralised service where decisions about courses were made within the competitive business environment of individual colleges and other training providers. Community education was weakened not only by temporary loss of funding, but through LEAs selling buildings that had been venues for community groups. Support for voluntary agencies, specialist teachers and training courses were dropped and networks that had been sustained by county or regional bodies fell away (Hamilton, 1997). The Special Development Funding that had been available from ALBSU for any LEA in the 1990s also became subject to competitive tendering and it was no longer possible to run the scheme in the same way. Some of the strongest networks that remained were those involved with validating and verifying student qualifications (see Martin, 1988).

There was a strong impetus towards accrediting provision to gain FEFC funding. There were large variations in the unit of funding, and programme organisers had to understand the intricacies of the funding mechanism to make best use of the funds available for the provision that they had and hoped to make in subsequent years. The projects that flourished did so through the skills and energy of practitioners who managed to combine multiple funding streams (see for example the Derbyshire cross-partnership project Read On Write Away! http://www.rowa.co.uk/).

In 1995 ALBSU became the Basic Skills Agency (BSA) with an extended remit for basic skills in schools. This supported its increasing involvement with family literacy. It no longer advocated solely for adults and this role was increasingly taken up by NIACE.

Phase 4 1998 to the present: Development of Skills for Life policy; New government strategy unit created; £1.5 billion of government money is committed

During this final period of our research, literacy and numeracy, including adult literacy, moved to a pivotal position within policy and within the discourses of human resource development and social inclusion.

In 1997, the era of Conservative government ended with the election of New Labour under Tony Blair. This was to signal a turning point for the field. A report from the Organisation for Economic Cooperation and Development (the OECD) on the findings from the International Adult Literacy Survey (IALS) showed the UK to be near the bottom of a new league table of industrial nations. Having put in place a new Literacy Strategy for schools, the New Labour government set up a review of adult basic skills in 1998, chaired by Sir Claus Moser. The Moser report, *A Fresh Start*, recommended a new Basic Skills strategy, referring to estimates from the International Literacy Survey that suggested seven million adults were in need of ALLN (see OECD, 1997). By 2001, *Skills for Life* had emerged as a cornerstone of the newly integrated Learning Skills sector. Basic skills were claimed to be crucial not only for employment, but – in line with New Labour's commitments to social inclusion and 'joined up government' – also to personal, family, citizenship and community participation (UNESCO, 1997; OECD, 1997, 2000; Kennedy, 1997; Tomlinson, 1996).

A new funding agency for post-school education and training, the Learning and Skills Council (LSC), was created in 2001, replacing the FEFC and local Training and Enterprise Councils (TECs). A new Adult Learning Inspectorate

(ALI) was created. Local Strategic Partnerships were encouraged to develop collaboration as a way of overcoming the competitive approach created under the previous funding regime.

The BSA, which had played a central role in the development of ALLN and the creation of the new strategy, was not given the steering role for *Skills for Life* in England. A new government strategy unit, The Adult Basic Skills Strategy Unit (ABSSU), was set up directly within the Department for Education and Skills (DfES), closely controlled and regulated by the Cabinet Office. The BSA took on a more restricted developmental role and its focus moved more strongly to schools and family literacy, though it retained responsibility for the adult literacy strategy in Wales.

In the new strategy, literacy, numeracy and ESOL are fully established as specialisms in their own right and ICT has been added as a fourth basic skill. ESOL was not initially distinguished within the strategy and ESOL activists and practitioners, such as representatives from the London Language and Literacy Unit (LLU), lobbied for this to happen. They were involved in the development of the ESOL curriculum, the creation of ESOL materials, the establishment of a programme of professional development and qualifications and the mapping of ESOL qualifications. This was an example of a successful policy intervention by activists to safeguard the interests of ESOL learners in the first nationally funded basic skills framework.

Core curricula for literacy, numeracy and ESOL, standards, a national test and new qualifications for learners and tutors were introduced in England in 2002. Targets were closely tied to funding, and to specific groups of adults. In line with an increased emphasis on evidence-based policy and practice, a National Research and Development Centre was set up (the NRDC), in which a number of universities and key policy oriented bodies collaborated. Most importantly, the Treasury made large amounts of money available for the new strategy together with a promotional campaign featuring the Gremlins on prime time television (see Chapter 10).

In the following chapters we describe a growing field of practice, full of tensions and competing discourses and moving from an 'invented space' into the mainstream. We examine how these tensions have been managed, how the discourses have influenced practice and how the pushing and pulling of a host of activists, agencies and government initiatives have influenced the field so that it has become the shape it is today.

2

Situating ourselves in the field:
a reflexive methodology

I didn't realise I could talk like this to be perfectly honest. I suppose what you
have made me realise is the fact that this is a fantastic job to do and it has
been 12 years where [I] have come into contact with so many inspiring staff.
Just talking about the names and thinking about all the students and you
know this is why I do it. I don't know ... what the phrase for that is but it just
seems to be quite inspiring really. (CW, Leicester P 55:1076)

How do you go about gathering a history of a field? Starting from a view
of literacy and numeracy as part of social practice, we wanted to create
a multi-voiced account that represents the different experiences of
those who have participated in ALLN. In this chapter, we set out our understanding of the social practice approach in relation to the methodological
choices we made. One of our aims, as expressed in the quote above, was to
generate new reflections on the field, not just to document existing knowledge.

What do we mean by social practice?
A social practice approach emphasises the uses, meanings and values of
reading, writing and numeracy in everyday activities, and the social relationships and institutions within which literacy is embedded. The social practice
approach is drawn upon by the New Literacy Studies (NLS) which has
developed over the last 20 years. It offers specific and detailed ethnographic
evidence about the way in which people learn through the written word, both
in and outside formal educational settings. There are several recent reviews
and edited collections that offer an overview of the main features of this body
of work. These include Barton *et al* (2000); Hodge (2003); Hull and Schultz

(2002); Street (1993, 2004). Martin-Jones and Jones (2000) review multilingual literacies; and Coben (2003) reviews numeracy.

This approach sees literacy, numeracy and language as part of social practices which are observable in 'events' or 'moments' and are patterned by social institutions and power relationships. This view encourages us to look beyond texts themselves to what people *do* with literacy and numeracy literacy, with whom, where, and how. It demands that we make connections: with the community in which learners lead their lives outside the classroom; with notions of situated learning; between learning and institutional power; between spoken language, print and other media; between the literacies and numeracies of teachers and researchers. The focus shifts from deficit or lack, to the many different ways that people engage with literacy and maths, recognising difference and diversity and challenging how these differences are valued within our society.

Literacy and numeracy, then, are shaped by the social and cultural context within which practice is embedded, the meanings it has for its users, and the purposes it serves. This approach leads us to view the three groups (policy actors, practitioners and learners) as overlapping but disparate communities who relate to policy initiatives of ALLN in different ways. Throughout this book we link policy with everyday practice, both within and outside educational settings.

What does this mean for our methodology?
It is not a big leap from this approach to the methodology we used in this study. We needed methods that would start from the assumption that the meanings of adult literacy, numeracy and language are constantly changing and that such changes will be associated with varying discourses, activities and organisational structures. We wanted a collaborative approach to research that engages in a dialogue with interviewees about how the field has been created and shaped. We needed methods that acknowledge that participants act in terms of their own understandings of literacy, numeracy and language. They improvise and use resources within inherited constraints as they make sense of a changing environment. Key events and moments that individuals identify are personal to them, but they can also be seen in relation to the bigger pattern of changes in the field.

Choosing a sample
England is a densely populated country, and in each of the 104 local education authorities (LEAs) there are adult and community learning centres,

further education colleges and a host of voluntary and employment-related learning organisations involved in the delivery of ALLN. We needed to choose a sample to represent this diverse provision as well as talking to people acknowledged as being key national players in shaping the field. We chose four case study areas in England:

- A northern urban area with a history of student writing, Manchester
- A county that had urban and rural areas and a community education structure, Leicestershire
- A rural area, Norfolk
- A London region, North East London

In addition, we worked with a few organisations that were interested in documenting their history. These included Pecket Well, a student-managed college near Halifax, and the Friends' Centre in Brighton, both of which had significant involvement with national events, and, in the latter case, had staff who progressed to influential careers in adult education or ALLN or related fields.

In order to identify people to interview, we initially drew on our existing networks and documents we knew of. As the interviews proceeded we gathered more recommendations. With the help of the Learning and Skills Development Agency we sent out around 2,000 copies of a short questionnaire, publicising the research and asking people if they wished to become involved. The responses to this publicity widened our range of contacts, and helped us to shape our interview questions and decide upon the case study sites.

We talked to people in each region whose roles were key to their local history, even if they had not been players on the national stage. We looked for a range of specialists in each area and for people working at different organisational levels. We conducted semi-structured interviews asking people to tell us how they had become involved in ALLN, and about their experiences of teaching, organising and management. We invited them to tell us about high points and low points in their careers, and to identify key moments, people and documents that they felt had influenced their practice and the field in general. The key events are often moments of tension or conflict that crystallise bigger underlying issues and we found it particularly useful to focus on these and the ways they have been managed.

We did not come to the interviews with blank slates but took a checklist of themes and prompts based on our existing knowledge and literature to help guide the conversation and later the analysis. There are a number of recognisable and competing discourses in the field and we explored a set of com-mon underlying issues: the views our interviewees held about learners, tutors, policy actors, the teaching and learning process, institutional con-texts, and the goals of the field.

In total, we carried out nearly 200 oral history interviews with decision-makers in a range of government and national agencies, and practitioners en-gaged in teaching and organising ALLN programmes. We also interviewed adults with basic skills needs, some of whom had been involved in formal learning. Our research has tried to capture the interactions between these groups and to identify whether, and in what ways, they have come to in-fluence the current central position of basic skills in the current government's learning agenda in England.

Doing oral history interviews

We see our work as a contribution to the field of popular oral history (Perks and Thomson, 1998). This approach to history was developing rapidly around the time of the *Right to Read* campaign in the 1970s, and significantly in-fluenced ALLN (Mace, 1979, 1998; O'Rourke, 2005).

Although we were asking people about the past, inevitably this was seen through the eyes of the present. We also captured, inadvertently, people's views about the current period of policy implementation from 2002-2004. Frisch (1998) suggests that oral history documents cannot be straightfor-wardly interpreted as 'factual' additions to the historical record, but they significantly add to it. They are documents of memory, showing the processes of selective remembering that are, as he puts it 'central in the way we all order our experience and understand the meaning of our lives'(Frisch, 1998: 37). Frisch suggests that three key questions can help unravel that complexity of oral history accounts: 'What sort of person is speaking?' 'What sort of thing is he or she talking about?' and 'What sort of statements about it are being made?' In particular, he makes a distinction between interviewees who are simply recounting their own experience, and those who are making generalisations about events of the time that they did not directly witness. What kinds of categories are they using to interpret and explain their ex-periences?

Oral history also helps us examine what Dorothy Holland has called the 'figured worlds' of our participants. A figured world is a socially produced and culturally constructed 'realm of interpretation' in which a particular set of characters and actors are recognised, significance is assigned to certain acts and particular outcomes are valued over others. Figured worlds are populated by a set of actors and agents who engage in a limited range of meaningful acts or changes in a particular situation. They are continuously figured in practice through the use of cultural artefacts or objects inscribed by the collective attribution of meaning (Bartlett and Holland, 2002, p12).

Where oral history is carried out with participants who have left little trace of their views and activities in the public record (such as students or part-time tutors), oral history also functions to counter the elitism of that record and to give voice to silenced groups (Popular Memory Group, 1998). This function of oral history motivated much of the movement toward student writing and community publishing that is described in Chapter 8.

In addition to oral interviews, we collected documents and created an archive from personal donations and materials gathered from the case study sites and national agencies. Historical records are typically uneven in the ways they represent the experience of different participants. Whilst this is true of ALLN, the record we have available is unusual in that we do have a large body of first-hand written autobiographic narratives by the adult learners themselves, the result of the tradition of student writing and community publishing that has been a unique feature of practice in the field since its beginnings in the 1970s. The whole point of the educational activities such as Writing Events that produced these accounts was to make visible a written record of the participants' experiences

A way to examine the changing use of language is through discourse analysis. Gee, Hull and Lankshear (1996) provides a useful definition for such an analysis:

> A Discourse is composed of ways of talking, listening, reading, writing, acting, interacting, believing, valuing and using tools and objects, in particular settings and at specific times, so as to display or to recognise a particular social identity ... The Discourse creates social positions (or perspectives) from which people are 'invited' ('summoned') to speak, listen, act, read and write, think, feel, believe, and value in certain characteristic, historically recognisable ways, in combination with their own individual style and creativity ... Discourses create, produce and reproduce opportunities for people to be and recognise certain *kinds of people* (Gee, Hull and Lankshear, 1996, p10, italic in original)

This, then, is why we have taken the trouble to examine people's ideas, their language, and the products of the activities in the form of archive material. We can see that our social practices approach allows us to examine the wider context in which people act. What people *do*, and what they refrain from *doing*, is also shaped by what the prevailing discourses allow. Discourse analysis, then, reveals something of the underpinning ideologies that shape peoples' thoughts, words and practices. As Hajer and Wagenaar put it:

> Organised systems of action and belief powerfully shape actors' understanding of complex social and technological situations to the extent that they form their own justification and drive other ways of doing or understanding outside the sphere of what is believed to be feasible or acceptable. Their foundation in the spontaneity of people's everyday activities makes their constraining influence on open democratic deliberation particularly insidious as they, in Bourdieu's felicitous phase, 'naturalise their own arbitrariness'. ... Practice theory goes beyond interpretation in that it stresses the sense (over the more cerebral meaning) of a situation. People who are engaged in a practice have assumed a particular social identify that they signal to their environment, and that validates what they do and say both to themselves and to the world at large. (Hajer and Wagenar, 2003:28)

Policy actors

We began by looking for a distinct group of people called 'policy makers'. Yeatman (2000), talks about 'policy activists' who operate through their networks at a number of different levels within the system to make a difference to the outcome of policy. Policy activists do not just carry out their work routinely, but pursue a particular vision of it across time and institutional boundaries. Such activists can be effective over long periods of time. They can intervene at any of the stages of the policy cycle described above: getting issues onto the policy agenda, facilitating communication with user groups, in or outside the institutional process, and maintaining the momentum of change.

We interviewed people who have always had a policy and strategic involvement in the field from the beginning of the 1970s, such as LEA officers, the director of the national agency for ALLN, the head of the Industrial Language Training Unit and some people involved in the media campaigns. But people who have been influential over a long period of time have usually played a number of different roles, typically moving from being a practitioner into positions where they could have some influence over policy and strategy. This may have been at the level of co-ordinator, principal of a college or adult education centre, as an advisor, inspector, committee member or officer in a LEA, or in terms of national agencies and organisations, such as becoming a regional development worker for ALBSU. Some learners also moved across roles, becoming volunteers and then paid tutors or activists in national organisations. Stories of policy action are therefore typically grounded in stories of practice from the same informant. There are no neat categories of 'policy maker' or 'practitioner' and for this reason we started thinking in terms of 'policy actors', who might operate at a variety of levels.

We encouraged everyone we interviewed to tell us their personal story of how they got involved with basic skills and what directions their career has taken. Most people were happy to be identified publicly with their real names and shared our aim of putting a range of stories into the historical record. Where we have drawn on the interview data in this book, we have used people's initials in the text and we list their full names in Appendix Three. In this sense there was a shared orientation and sense of purpose to the interviews, regardless of the positions people hold, or have held in the field. However, it was also clear that some people were not just telling a personal account of their career, but were speaking as representatives of an organisation to which they are held accountable (Walford, 1994). They are powerful, public figures in their own right, with responsibilities to others they work with and lines of argument for which they are mouth pieces. The accounts they offer for public consumption will necessarily remain partial with a more personal off the record version very seldom heard. We interviewed a lot of people as they were at the point of retiring or changing position and this is important to record as it affected the degree to which they felt free to present their story and how they looked back on their career at different points.

Paying attention to the features of the interview exchange helps reveal these complexities. Ball (1994) talks about the detail of question and answer, the different styles in which people respond, withhold information and take hold of the direction of the interview to understand the particular rule of the game that is being played out in different encounters. For politicians and civil servants these games are quite deliberate and form part of their knowledge about what they can or cannot speak about directly. One possible strategy is for the interviewer to challenge the game (for example by being well-prepared beforehand and asking questions that s/he knows will provoke discussion). The aim of such interviews is not necessarily to push for the 'real facts' but to gain a detailed and reflective version of the informant's perspective.

Practitioners' perspectives

The majority of our interviews with practitioners were conducted on an individual basis, where we asked people to tell us about how they joined the field, their views about the learners, about other practitioners, who was a 'key' person from their perspective, what key moments stood out for them, and highs and lows of working in ALLN. We also conducted some group interviews. Here, we started by showing them a sample of one person's memories of events from each decade, with dates where recollected. We encouraged practitioners to draw upon their 'fuzzy' memories by asking them to write down any event that they felt was important and worth sharing with the best estimate of when that event occurred. Each event was written on a sticky yellow label. These were then posted on a large flipchart paper, one for each decade. As people wrote down their memories, they tended to talk about them and this dialogue invariably led to the prompting of more memories and fine tuning some of the haziness around dates. We often found that people could date the events in relation to their personal lives, such as the birth of a child, moving house or changing jobs. The collected events helped us create our timelines, and provided an indication of how important an event was to that particular group of practitioners, and often to the field generally. We invited practitioners to bring their own artefacts and these, too, prompted discussion.

Sometimes practitioners wanted their identities protected because of being vulnerable in their employment. They inevitably talked to us through the lens of their current position and pre-occupations. They had difficult as well as positive things to say about the past. They varied greatly on how far they were able or willing to reflect on the bigger picture rather than simply recount their own experiences.

Learners' perspectives

When we were designing our study, we felt the learners would be the most difficult group to sample and fully represent. Most adults who have expressed needs for support in ALLN, or who have been assessed as needing such help, have not taken part in formal adult education during the period we have studied. Most of those adults who *have* taken part have moved through ALLN to other things, and for many of them it will have been a fleeting even if significant part of their lives. For these reasons we chose to interview a sample of adults from a longitudinal study, the National Child Development Survey (NCDS), comprising people who were born in one particular week in March 1958.

The NCDS cohort members have been subject to surveys at different times throughout their lives. Of the original 17,000 members, there are approximately 12,000 still in the survey. In 1981, when they were young adults, they were asked as part of the survey if they felt they had difficulty with literacy or numeracy, and from this number it was estimated how many people in the country may have this problem. A ten percent sample of the whole cohort was subsequently asked to take part in literacy and numeracy tests, and this produced a higher estimate of need.

We chose a sample of people, all of whom fell within the target group for the *Skills for Life* strategy. We structured the sample on the basis of their test results, their self-reported literacy and/or numeracy difficulties and their interest in taking part in formal learning. We limited the sample to cohort members who currently live as near as possible to our case study sites and we completed 78 out of a target of 100 interviews. This group of people are now in their mid-40s, and were young adults at the time of the initial literacy campaign. We could ask about their own experiences of learning, and if they are aware of and have engaged with learning opportunities to improve their basic skills. The interviews we carried out with these people enabled us to look beyond the world of adult education and to present some evidence about the perspectives and everyday lives of non-participants in relation to literacy and numeracy.

In our interviews with the NCDS cohort members, we were interested to discover how they made use of literacy and numeracy in their everyday lives, and if they experienced any of the disruptions which would be predicted from the statistical profiles of the cohort in relation to health, educational success and careers (Ferri *et al*, 2003). We asked about their family and wider social networks, what had been happening since their last interview, what they knew about learning opportunities in their area, what learning they had undertaken, both formally and informally, and whether they remembered any of the media campaigns promoting ALLN. We discussed their experiences of new technologies and their views of the current learning environment experienced by their own children and grandchildren. People re-evaluated their strengths and skills during the interviews, and their views of what counts as learning.

Working with the NCDS cohort members imposed a set of practical research challenges that were different from the rest of the interviews. The survey offered us extensive background information about the people we interviewed, but in turn we had to respect existing protocols for anonymity and contact procedures so as not to jeopardise relationships that had been built up over many years.

Creating an archive

We asked people to donate materials and documentation for an archive, which we have gathered for future researchers to make use of. People up and down the country pulled out boxes stored in their lofts and garages, in cupboards in community centres and on bookshelves in libraries, with copies of materials and learning resources they made, or books they used, and even floppy discs from obsolescent computer hardware. This archive is being collated and systematically recorded on a website that was created for the project, so that anyone who is interested can find out what we have gathered, and can eventually make use of it once it is stored at Lancaster University.

What we do not have, of course, is a full, representative sample of all the material outputs over the past three decades. Technologies change, and some electronic material is already inaccessible. In between the sheaves of papers in our archive there are old tapes, reels of microfiche and film of unknown specifications. Without the original machines that produced these items, their content is locked away in plastic and metal. Paper based artefacts become ragged, incomplete, and in some cases, are simply dumped when offices are moved, and institutions merged or disbanded. Institutional memory is very susceptible to these losses, and we are aware of the fragmentary nature of our material and the sense that we, acting as historians, can make of it.

The extent of technological change since the 1970s is brought home vividly through the documents we have collected. They already look antiquated. The paper itself has aged, but even official documents like government memos are typewritten rather than computer-generated. Homemade logos are stuck and pasted, title pages created with Letraset. Teaching materials are cut by hand, handwritten or typed. There are smudged carbon copies, duplicated using purple or turquoise ink of the Banda machine or badly photocopied and skewed on shiny paper.

New technologies have changed the standards of neatness and professionalism we expect from a text, in particular the use of computers both to wordprocess and to type-set publications. Later material shows a more flexible layout and contains many more images and graphics. Multi-media texts are common.

Analysing the data
The data consisted of transcripts of interviews and background notes, boxes of archive material and records of project meetings. Data analysis was iterative, and began as we collected the data. We used a grounded theory approach (as in Glaser and Strauss, 1967; Strauss and Corbyn, 1990), moving between theory and data. We would undertake some interviews, read, discuss

and edit the transcripts. Subsequent interviews were informed by what had gone before.

We were analysing a complex field in relation to policy, organisational change and an emerging practice which is located in a much wider arena of social action. We needed to look at the data at a number of levels to do justice to this complexity. We used chronological time as a central organising framework, juxtaposing the public with the personal and more local timelines. We analysed developments at international, national, regional and local levels. We tracked individual life histories or trajectories for people or organisations. We looked at the discourse as well as the content of people's accounts.

Developing timelines

As we collected archive material and documentary evidence from local and national policymaking, donations from participants and responses to our website requests, and interview transcripts, we started to create a series of timelines across the three decades. These show specific events which we dated from public records, and the personal memories of our respondents. The timeline formed a backbone against which our history of ALLN was fleshed out. Within the central timelines are thematic timelines. For example, we developed a media timeline, which focuses on campaigns to inform the public about basic skills issues, starting with the original BBC *On the Move* campaign.

Thematic analysis

Once we had gathered the interview and documentary evidence and began constructing our timelines, we had an enormous amount of material to make sense of. Creating some order over this data is always an activity of interpretation and construction. Possibly the most challenging for us was how to analyse policy which we will talk about in Chapter 3. We started the analysis with the codes and categories we had used to design the interviews, such as accreditation and professional development, issues of motivation, how participants construed the field, their views about the teaching and learning process and the goals of ALLN. We also worked from the data itself to identify further categories, allowing the data to speak for itself. For example, we had originally expected to find policy throughout the three decades we were studying, either at national or local level. We soon realised, however, that policy directly aimed at a national level, apart from the early flurry during the 1970s campaign, did not exist until much later in the 1990s. At the same time, we began to identify very clear periods within the timeline. Much later, a set of enduring tensions emerged that were formulated and managed differently through the three decades in an environment of rapid change. By allowing the data to speak for itself, through the multiple voices that we had gathered, we continually refined our framework of analysis.

We used a software programme, *Atlas-Ti*, to analyse our data. This software enabled us to create codes based on our initial interests and add those which we identified by undertaking analyses of a number of transcripts and moderating these as a team. We could draw together groups of codes into families, we could analyse groups of transcripts by any number of characteristics, for example by case study area, by practitioner or by learner, and we could search for codes which were particularly frequent. We identified codes which related to views held about the nature of ALLN and views held about other actors in the field from the interviewees such as learners, practitioners and volunteers. We had a second level of analysis, where we were beginning to identify tensions. We used the codes to structure our emergent thinking as well as to capture the data. We could search systematically across the data for instances of the codes and for key words related to them. Sometimes this resulted in saturated categories, where the same story or theme recurred so frequently throughout the interviews that we felt that we could predict and explain the next response as it fell into the same pattern. We wrote notes to each other, using memos attached to codes. We created a log of the issues we needed to address, recording how our own thinking about the meaning of the transcripts changed over a two-year period.

Discourse analysis

The language of basic skills has changed during the past three decades. Discourse analysis is time-consuming and focuses intensively on small samples of data. In this book we are only able to refer in a limited way to what we did. We chose a selection of policy documents from different points from the 1970 onward and used a critical discourse analysis approach (Wodak, 2001; Fairclough, 2003) to examine the ways they presented ALLN as a social policy problem and how learners, practitioners and policy actors were constructed through both text and images. We searched for similar discourse features in the interviews and, in addition, noted hesitations, the use of humour, metaphors and interviewees' comments about the nature of memory and their feelings about trying to recall events from the far-away past.

A resource for future research

The understandings that we have arrived at from our research are necessarily our own and we know that there are many other takes on our data. The data itself is a selection, reflecting our interests and research questions. As the following chapters will show, the bigger picture can be drawn in a number of ways. The different groups of people we talked to bring a variety of cultures and experiences to the data and their reflections and realities emphasise particular themes that we could discern in the data. People who are new to the field of basic skills will have their own stories to tell, revealing further perspectives on ALLN.

The documents and interview transcripts we have gathered are available for future research and interpretation. In particular, others may find that they can make use of these to search for particular themes that we have not yet identified or had time to deal with in any depth. For example, a history of the way in which learning resources have been created, and the influences of technology on these, would make an important contribution to the way in which learners are supported today. Other analyses can be undertaken, based on our work. Our data provides the opportunity for practitioners to challenge their current position within the *Skills for Life* strategy, seeing it within the context of a much wider and longer-lasting social project.

Readers can consult our archive database for further information on what is held there. The archive can be accessed on-line at http://litcent.lancs.ac.uk/RIS/RISWEB.ISA

The Changing Faces website is at http://literacy.lancs.ac.uk/links/changing faces.htm

Our website also has anonymised samples of the interview data, more details about project activities and the methods we used to prompt memories and reflections on ALLN. These methods can easily be adapted for use with enquiry groups whether these are groups of friends and colleagues, a classroom setting with adult learners, a professional development session with tutors new to the field, or a mixed group of policy actors, practitioners and learners exploring an issue together.

3

Top down or bottom up?
The search for policy action

Introduction

As we described in Chapter 1, for much of the period we have studied, the field of ALLN has developed in the margins of post-compulsory education and training. Participation in lifelong learning has remained stubbornly in favour of those best qualified from initial schooling (see Sargant, 2000; Kennedy, 1997). However, with the election of the New Labour government in 1997, for the first time ALLN became the focus of a co-ordinated national policy strategy pursued with the energy and managerialist rationality that has come to characterise the Blair administration. Following the review of adult basic skills (Moser, 1999), the government in England introduced a *Skills for Life* strategy (SK4L), with substantial funding. SK4L created a national curriculum for learners, a dedicated basic skills qualification structure and a set of professional standards to which practitioners must adhere. Each aspect of the strategy has achievement and participation targets.

How did the field of ALLN gain such government interest and what were the significant mechanisms or factors in this process? The central focus of our study is on change, and this must partly be explained through an analysis of national governance and policy. The state has a number of powerful tools at its disposal to affect social policy if the political will is present. Burns (1961) identifies four different kinds of power that can be exerted by state agencies to influence change: direct coercion; financial incentives and penalties; normative pressure and access to knowledge. These kinds of power are enforced variously through legislation; funding and audit and performance indicators; social networks, structures of consultation and decision-making and discourses.

However, central government does not always recognise problems that might be actively addressed or is not interested in pushing policy forward in a particular area. This has been the case with ALLN and, while the field has certainly changed, this has happened without a co-ordinated national policy for much of the period since the 1970s. We therefore needed to look at theories of change more generally and at how, or whether, change is managed. Whilst much of the literature about change is framed at the level of organisational theory and design rather than macro level social processes, the approaches it describes show parallels with approaches in the policy analysis literature and, indeed, Parsons (1995) identifies a strong link between policy analysis and management science with its interest in how decisions come to be made (by elite groups or pluralistically; rationally or incrementally).

In line with the social practice approach to literacy and numeracy we described earlier, we need an approach to policy analysis that situates ALLN in the context of everyday communicative practices. We favour an approach that sees policy as a social project that constructs and frames a social problem (in this case ALLN) and which shows how that social project gains momentum is realised and stabilised, rather than discovering it ready-made. We need an approach that can take account of the perspectives of the heterogeneous actors and interest groups that contribute to the development of the field and the complex, lived realities experienced by these participants. Our approach must also be able to take account of an environment of competing social policy projects whose agendas may sometimes support and sometimes be in tension with ALLN.

This chapter sets out a framework for policy analysis that fits the field and could help explain the history of change in ALLN. The framework takes elements from a number of writers, especially Hajer and Wagenaar (2003), who put forward a notion of 'deliberative policy analysis' where practice is taken as the unit of analysis.

Approaches to public policy analysis

Policies do not normally tell you what to do; they create circumstances in which the range of options available in deciding what to do are narrowed or changed. A response must still be put together, constructed in context, offset against other expectations. All of this involves creative social action, not robotic reactivity. (Ball, 1993:12)

Ball (1993) and Parsons (1995) consider policy analysis to be essentially a 'boot-strapping activity' where no one theory or model is adequate to explain the complexity of the policy activity of the modern state. In this view, analysis of public policy involves the 'appreciation of the network of ideas, concepts and words which form the world of explanation within which policy-making and analysis takes place (Parsons, 1995:73). Ball suggests we need a 'toolbox' of diverse concepts and theories (Ball, 1993:10). Following this suggestion, we have drawn upon four approaches that we could identify from the literature on policy action and change:

1. A neat view of a linear rational process
2. A messy view of the push and pull of multiple, conflicting perspectives
3. A critical view, emphasising discursive struggles for power and legitimacy
4. A deliberative policy view which sees policy as being made through networks engaged in everyday debate and interaction

Each has something to offer, and each is limited in particular ways.

The first approach suggests that policy making should be seen as a linear, rational process which attempts to solve problems scientifically (Simon, 1957; Dror, 1967). A number of writers have suggested 'stagist' approaches to analysis (see for example May and Wildavsky, 1978) where policy can be followed as it reaches the agenda; becomes formulated and refined; defines the problem; is implemented, changed and leads to new policy formation.

Although policymaking in ALLN has not been composed of such 'tidy, neat steps phases or cycles' (Parsons, 1995:79), the search for chronological stages or phases can be a useful heuristic device that helps manage the sheer complexity of the data. For this reason, we decided to look for policy phases as one starting point for structuring our analysis, searching for events and documents which could be reconstructed in a public timeline. The four policy phases we outlined in Chapter 1 demonstrate shifting power between different agencies and the individuals who work within them. In these key phases, it is clear that there are flurries of policy making, and even longer periods where little activity was apparent. The policy moments often relate to the wider economic climate, and have been influenced by key political speeches.

The creation of a policy does not always lead to implementation. If it does, the policy may be subverted, diverted or ignored by those responsible for enacting it. Once policy has been created, changes continue to be made to the stabilised problem even though these may not be controlled by the original policymakers. Policy may drift or be neglected due to other, more pressing demands on government. There are also policy lacunae: gaps where there is no policy activity, even though there are emerging issues.

A second group of policy analysts, then have pointed out that policy processes are messy and politically highly charged. They involve negotiation and mediation between multiple conflicting interests. They may not be informed by rational argument or draw upon research evidence prior to creation and implementation. They may be a response to activists or to media revelations. Policy-making is not solely top-down but agency is exerted at many levels, including what Lipsky called the 'street level bureaucrats' who translate policy at the front-line of interactions with the users of policy (in our case, the practitioners) (Lipsky, 1979; and see also Elmore, 1985).

This second approach emphasises the importance of researching the perspectives of a variety of actors positioned at all levels of the policy process, all of whom may exert some agency within the field. Yeatman (1998) offers some useful distinctions between a number of levels where policy action may take place:

- Public servants responsible for turning general policy directions into operational policy, then into programme management, and to co-ordinate with any NGOs involved.
- Service providers who deliver policy on the ground.
- Potential and actual users of policy.
- Those who give evaluative feedback on policy, including professional evaluators, citizens, lobbying groups and political parties.
- Those who enforce due process and legislation.
- Those involved with monitoring and auditing policy.

This view of change suggests that we may find alternative views and definitions of the 'problem' of ALLN from the different actors involved. It may also help us explain how the field can change in the absence of top-down policy initiatives

A third group of critical policy analysts have developed argumentative and discursive approaches which focus on how language and culture shape the way in which we make sense of the world and the possibilities we see for action within it. The language we use is not neutral, and therefore the way in which policy making occurs can be examined in terms of narrative and discourse as it develops through a 'never ending series of communications and strategic moves by which various policy actors in loosely coupled forums of public deliberation construct inter-subjective meanings' (Hoppe, 1993:77).

This third model is consistent with our notion of literacy as social practice and helpful to our research, as it gives voice to those who are often silenced by more conventional policy analyses, as well as the key actors in the field. Interview data from different people can be combined and contrasted using critical discourse analysis and put side by side with other documentary, statistical and other sources.

This approach reveals the ways in which a problem is temporarily stabilised to make it into a tractable project for social policy action (Law, 1994; Lo Bianco, 2001; Fowler, 2004). When a problem is stabilised in this way, tensions inevitably occur as practitioners and other actors in the field find themselves being pulled by different agendas in the social policy area. For example, as we show in Chapter Five, practitioners are influenced by the vocational agenda, the wider benefits of learning and the quality agenda, all three acting as forces upon the evolving landscape of practice in the field. This suggests that we will find long-term tensions that different stakeholder groups have to manage on the basis of their own lived experience and understandings. These tensions can be influenced by a number of different organisations, each affecting the field of ALLN with its own remit, perspectives and level of influence. Inherent within a critical approach to policymaking is the understanding that some discourses are privileged and define how problems are construed and consequently how resulting action is permitted (Wodak and Meyer, 2001).

We found a fourth approach, deliberative policy analysis, to be most useful of all. Hajer and Wagenaar (2003) claim that the complexity of any public activity necessarily involves networks of people including those who make policy, those who argue for it to be made, and those who deal on a day-to-day basis with the issue being addressed. Ambiguities and uncertainties in the field of ALLN, as with any other area of public activity, contain taken for granted practices which need to be articulated if policymaking is to be successful. Like others mentioned above, Hajer and Wagenaar recognise that there are multiple actors with different investments and resources in the field. They argue that people's engagement in policy enactment is

...fuelled and expressed in their passions and feelings about certain situations. They harbour sympathies and antipathies toward the people that
make up their world. They are strongly committed to some subjects and in-
different and apathetic towards others.. as a consequence, policy issues are,
almost by definition, contested. Moreover, resources of money and power
are differentially distributed among the actors involved. (Hajer and Wagenaar,
2003: 21)

Their approach, deliberative policy analysis (DPA), enables us to address our
basic question of how policy has shaped the field of ALLN. Hajer and
Wagenaar suggest that there is a 'widespread dissatisfaction with the limited
reach of 'set solutions' to thorny political issues imposed through top-down
government intervention' (p5). They go on to argue that in modern society,
particularly with the use of new communication technologies, people are
networked in a diverse and increasing number of ways, and this means that
they can participate in an expansive democracy by means of small-scale
direct democracy or through strong linkages between citizens and broad-
scale institutions. This means that democracy is pushed beyond its traditional political spheres, and decision-making relates more closely to the
people who are affected. Under such conditions, Hajer and Wagenaar suggest
that policy analysis should focus on concrete *manifestations* of policymaking
and politics such as the setting up of interest groups within and outside
formal constituencies. Once we think about people who are involved in a
much more active way in policy making (see also Yeatman, 1998), we can see
that politics and policymaking are not simply about finding solutions for
pressing problems, but also about finding formats for social policy action that
enlist and generate trust among mutually interdependent actors (Hajer and
Wagenaar, 2003:12).

The view presented by Hajer and Wagenaar is a highly normative one. It not
only describes the role of dispersed networks, but prescribes how best to engage the diverse actors in the field. It asserts that people who are involved on
a day-to-day basis with any particular problem are highly knowledgeable
about their situation and need to be included in the policymaking process in
a much more open and democratic way. Decisions and networks outside
formal institutions can be an important part of determining the policy process. This results in an approach to policy that focuses on everyday lives,
practices and interactions. In concrete, everyday situations, people create
meaning out of their behavioural dispositions or, in the vocabulary of Hajer
and Wagenaar (2003), by participating in practices:

> Practitioners of very different plumage wrestle with conflict, power, uncertainty and unpredictability. Solutions are not so much formulated as arrived at, haltingly, tentatively, through acting upon the situation at hand and through the application of practical wisdom in negotiating concrete situations ... (Hajer and Wagenaar, 2003:19)

This reformulated, deliberative policy science therefore takes *practices* as its unit of analysis and, in this way, it fits well with the historical approach to literacy studies we outlined in Chapter Two. Its task, Hajer and Wagenaar argue, is to reveal the hidden ambiguity and uncertainties in the taken for granted policy practices and discourse, with the purpose of creating reflexive space for deliberation of issues, which itself contributes to the policy process appropriate to current conditions that hold within our networked society. It holds that organisational culture is important to consider in this process, though hard to manage, since unpredictable meanings and interpretations are involved.

This policy analysis framework seems to fit with the overall approach we have taken in our research (see Chapter Two and the beginning of this chapter), of exploring the multiple meanings of practices and interactions that our three overlapping groups of respondents are engaged in. It means that we can look for change agents; we can look for debates, conflicts and tension, for faltering steps to work with problems that are 'wicked', intractable and yet temporarily stabilised long enough to attempt a solution. We will expect failure and disagreement as well as successes in this process, because ultimately the problem is both shifting, dynamic and probably insoluble. We have therefore tried to capture the history of ALLN through paying attention to the conflicts, tensions and actions of the people involved and affected in the field, using a stagist approach, with deliberative policy analysis as our framework.

Deliberative policy analysis is a useful tool, not only for looking at current and future practice but, because it is a normative approach, we can use it as a yardstick to look through our data for activities that we would consider to have been effective. If, as Hajer and Wagenaar assert, deliberative judgements are the bedrock of policy and these emerge through collective, interactive discourse, the telling and re-telling of stories (or, as Holland and Lave (2001) would say 'creating figured worlds') then we can explore how far and in what ways this has happened in ALLN. Where in our data do we get a sense of the policy process? What stories do people tell us about this? What spaces for discussion, reflection and action have been available to people at different points between 1970s and the present and how have they moved into these spaces? What access have people had to the world of official policy-making?

We can look for the existence of local actions, whether and how far they were successful and offer insights to the field as it continues to influence and be influenced by public policymaking (Sanguinetti, 1999).

As we have shown in Chapter 1, policymaking does not occur in a vacuum and we believe that, as a fragmented and marginal field of policy and practice, ALLN has been particularly susceptible to influence from other social policy initiatives. In this book, we offer clear evidence of connections between the developments in the field of ALLN and broader political and cultural changes at national and international level. For example, wider debates and conflicts about the vocationalisation of education are manifested in key moments of change described by our informants. A specific example for ESOL shows how government legislation had far-reaching consequences, particularly for those providing language tuition for the workforce. The first Race Relations Act was really important to the policy of the formation of the whole of ESOL, as it made discrimination on grounds of race illegal for employers. There was

> a rising awareness of the need to address the really amazingly high levels of racism which existed at that time in employment (TJ, London).

The Department of Employment set up the Race Relations Employment Advisory Service with a dozen people, one in each region of the country, to persuade employers to take positive initiatives. The Race Relations Act influenced the Home Office and the Department for Employment to agree comparatively generous funding for provision for the Industrial Language Training Units (ILTUs). Later, however, it was also the national policy context of the Thatcher years which led to their demise, as public services came under scrutiny and funding was cut.

Doing deliberative policy analysis

We can analyse our critical history of ALLN by searching for the concrete manifestations of policymaking such as government reports, legislation and setting up of agencies, but also for the more abstract silences and the predictable tensions experienced by actors from the various networks and groups outlined in Chapter Two. In ALLN, policy influences have been brought to bear on a field which is not homogenous, and has long-standing debates about the function and purposes of ALLN, as many of our respondents recognised and articulated. We would expect to find different expressions of the problem of ALLN, and different solutions and activities to deal with it, as we can now see that what can exist is partly defined through discourse, as well as through the direct exercise of coercive power and control. Our approach to analysis is shown in the diagram below (Figure 3.1). It offers us five lenses that

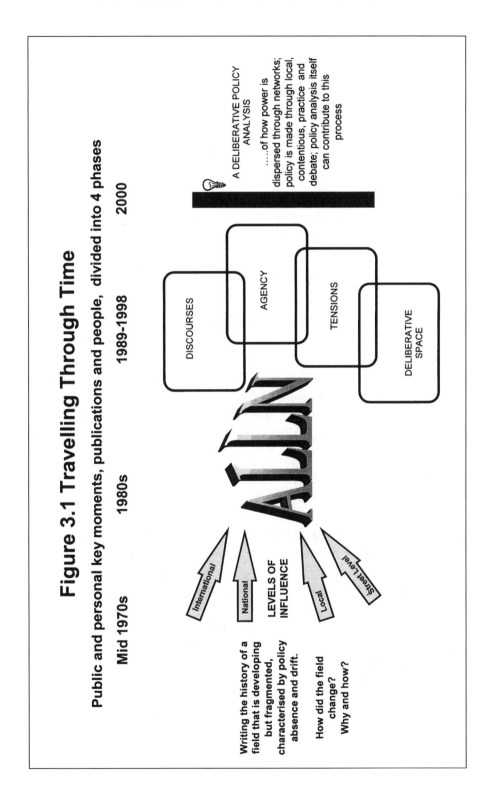

Figure 3.1 Travelling Through Time

Public and personal key moments, publications and people, divided into 4 phases

we can use to examine different aspects of ALLN. We describe these below, illustrating them with the example of *assessment* in the field of ALLN, a theme we deal with fully in Chapter Nine.

Lens one: *TIME*

We identify chronological trajectories in the policy process, some aspects of which can be reconstructed in a public timeline of events and documents. In particular, we look for

- Policy formation: how a problem is framed, how it reaches the policy agenda and how it is formulated as a practical strategy.
- Policy implementation, from the perspectives of the range of interested actors
- Policy review and feedback mechanisms, monitoring and consultation processes.

We can look and see how these processes happened, if at all in ALLN. We recognise that it is not always possible to clearly identify discrete policy cycles, and that such cycles may be punctuated by periods of policy drift or neglect within which change continues, but is not steered coherently from above. We assume that these processes are all highly politically charged and therefore not necessarily straightforwardly informed by research evidence or rational argument. However, it is possible to examine where agency lies at the different stages of the cycle.

We can map these phases by anchoring them to documents and events in our public timelines – the things that underpin the surface policy narrative. In each chapter we have included a thematic timeline, assembled from all our sources of data, to illustrate and reveal the policy narratives over time. So, for example, in looking at the development of assessment in the field, we look for significant moments, people, policy initiatives and publications related to this issue, mentioned in the literature and in the interview data. We assemble a timeline charting these and note how they fit against the four general phases we have identified in our overall timeline.

Lens two: *DISCOURSES*

For each policy phase or timeline, we can identify and analyse public discourses that have framed and stabilised the problem of ALLN at different points, and search for voices and silences. We will do this through discourse analysis of key documents and accounts from key people.

So, in relation to assessment, we can look at key policy and practitioner publications, such as the ALBSU newsletters, for the construction of issues
around measuring progress, testing outcomes and learner achievements, the
introduction of formal accreditation (initially through Wordpower and
Numberpower) and alternative approaches, such as through Open Colleges.
We can look at the surrounding policy context in which these issues were discussed, especially the rise of competency-based qualifications and pressures
toward accountability that were more general features of educational policy
during this period. In the most recent phase, we will look at the influence of
international testing through the OECD on how the problem of assessment
and evidence of achievement became seen in the field.

Lens three: AGENCY

For each phase, we can focus on the sources of agency in the field. We can
identify the actors and voices working across international, national, regional
and local levels, and examine how these levels interrelate in our data. In doing this, we will draw on both our analysis of the public timelines and the
interviews with diverse actors including practitioners and learners. Some
networks exist only at a local level, whilst others extend between and across
regions, localities and even nations. For example, there are voluntary
organisations, such as Blackfriars Settlement in London and the Friends'
Centre in Brighton, which have relationships with their LEA, the local adult
education service as well as with national agencies such as the Basic Skills
Agency. We see these organisations as being at 'street level' and the managers
and organisers who become involved in local, regional and national policy
making are therefore the 'street level bureaucrats' (in the sense discussed by
Lipsky, 1979). This also fits with Yeatman's idea of policy activism as working
throughout the field.

We will examine the ways that national policy impacts on such local contexts
and on individuals, drawing on the material identified by Lens 2. So, in
relation to assessment we will search for and compare the perspectives expressed by practitioners and policy actors in a variety of positions.

Lens four: TENSIONS

In each of our phases, we can now identify where tensions have arisen, how
they have been managed by policy actors, practitioners and learners in any
particular policy area, and we look to our public timelines and interview
material to reveal these tensions, conflicts and stories of how they have been
managed. Tensions around the issue of assessment are particularly salient in

the accounts we have. They relate to practitioners' views about the benefits and constraints of standardisation, student-centred approaches to teaching and learning, and to the diversity of the student body. As pressures toward more formal assessment have increased, practitioners and policy actors have had to engage with these tensions in more and more overt ways.

Lens five: DELIBERATIVE SPACE

Finally, we can examine the availability and distribution of deliberative, re-flexive space to engage with the issues we have identified as well as the actions that people undertook when this space was absent. Again, we draw upon our interview data to help us examine the policy process from the perspective of the imagined spaces and potential for change. Whereas, in the earlier historical phases, practitioners were often involved in discussing and developing new assessment procedures and a range of approaches existed side by side, the arrival of Wordpower and Numberpower at the end of the 1980s was seen by many as being imposed on the field by the Basic Skills Agency without formal consultation. The introduction of a national test for literacy and numeracy was controversial among policy-makers themselves and was discussed at length within the Moser committee. However, it was never put out for consultation with practitioners, in contrast to many other aspects of the *Skills for Life* strategy.

In the chapters that follow, we first take up aspects of the story from the perspective of the three key groups of people in our research: practitioners, policy actors and adult learners. We go on to examine a set of emerging themes which we identify as being particularly strong in their influence on the practice of ALLN. For each key group and theme we apply each of the lenses outlined above, asking questions and seeking evidence which may provide answers, or help define the silences, the lacunae and the yet to be imagined possible alternatives.

PART TWO

4

The learners

When literacy first became public in the mid-seventies a lot of figures were quoted on how many people could not read and write, but left blank 'Who are these X million people and where are they?' (John Glynn, in Gatehouse Books, 1983 p.5)

They put you to the back of the class and sort of just dismissed you. Well, you couldn't do it any way, so you didn't' try ... by the time I got to eleven I felt as if I wasn't capable of doing anything ... I just used to think nobody cares about me, nobody wants me. (Cath Newsham, Gatehouse Books, p.15-17)

Introduction

What were the prevalent discourses about adult learners of literacy, numeracy and ESOL at different points in time? What have they said about themselves, their experiences of formal learning and the ways they learn and communicate in everyday life? Many of the adults who might benefit from courses in literacy, numeracy or language have never taken part in basic skills provision since they left school. One important story, therefore, is about how these people deal with the challenges of living with limited literacy and numeracy skills in a textually mediated world, whether ALLN does indeed have anything to offer them and, if so, what might be done to attract them into educational programmes. We review evidence about everyday numeracy and literacy practices to find insights into these questions.

There is more speculation and opinion about who ALLN learners are, more first-hand testimony and anecdote about their characteristics and aspirations than there are hard facts and figures. Much of what we know – or think we know – about students, and potential students, comes from representations of them through the eyes of researchers, broadcasters, tutors and policy actors in policy documents and media programmes designed to advocate for funding and the expansion of provision. These representations tell us as much about the concerns and preconceptions of the times as they do about the students themselves. After the evaluation of the initial literacy campaign, funding for national research was largely spent on repeated efforts to demonstrate the extent of need (e.g. Hamilton and Stasinopoulos, 1987; Ekinsmyth and Bynner, 1994; Bynner and Steedman, 1995; Parsons and Bynner, 1999) and little on the experiences and aspirations of the people already in provision. Many small-scale research studies did accumulate, however, some conducted by practitioners (e.g. Mace, 1979; Clarke, 1989; Moss, 1988; Sanders, undated; Abell, 1992) and some with the participation of learners themselves (e.g. Cambridge House, 1984; Mace and Moss, 1988; Merry, 1984; Blackfriars Literacy Scheme, 1988). Reports from LEAs and ALBSU Special Development Projects sometimes documented the experience of learners (Charnley and Withnall, 1989).

There is a body of autobiographical writing generated by adults, in writing groups and community publishing (see Chapter 8). We have used these sources throughout this chapter as well as quotations from the interviews we carried out with adults from the NCDS that offer the perspective of non-participants in ALLN.

What's known about adult learners? Who and how many people

Statistics that are used to campaign for adult literacy language and numeracy have always been based on questionable estimates (see Chapter One). Patterns of actual participation in educational programmes at different phases since the 1970s have not been fully documented. Table 4.1 shows the information we have assembled, starting with participation in literacy programmes before the *Right To Read* campaign (see also Hamilton and Merrifield, 1999). This table shows a clear increase in programme enrolment from the initial campaign onwards. In the early stages of the *Right To Read* campaign, few systematic records of participation were collected. Jones and Charnley's evaluation of the adult literacy campaign (1978), was unable to put together a statistically representative sample of students. Hargreaves (1980) provides us with a meticulous record of student referrals from the BBC *On The Move* broadcasts (discussed in more detail in Chapter 10) but not all of these enrolled as students. By October 1978, after three years of campaigning,

---

Table 4.1: Participation in ALLN across the years

1972   A survey of local authority provision showed that just 5,000 adults were receiving help with reading and writing in England and Wales (Haviland, 1973)

1976   15,000 adults were receiving tuition across England and Wales (ALRA,1976)

1985   ALBSU estimated 110,000 adults receiving tuition in literacy, numeracy and ESOL (ALBSU, 1985)

1995-6 BSA reported that 319,402 people were receiving tuition in England, two-thirds of whom were studying in the FE sector.

2003-4 DfES 2004 reported that 639,000 learners had undertaken at least one S4L learning opportunity

---

50,000 students and 20,500 volunteer tutors had been referred to local schemes through the telephone hotline and enquiries were coming in at the rate of 200-300 per week. 57 per cent of the student referrals were men.

ALBSU collected monitoring statistics (omitting gender distributions and learning contexts). During the 1990s the FEFC collected more systematic figures for the two-thirds of ALLN learners who were now in FE colleges. Current statistics collected by the Learning Skills Councils, focused on learning outcomes, still do not enable easy estimates of participation to be made (Bathmaker, 2005).

The incomplete information reflects the diversity of contexts for adult learning, the many ways ALLN is embedded in other programmes, and the fragmented and sporadic nature of adult participation. We know that the numbers of people on the Manpower Services Commission (MSC) funded full-time TOPS and pre-TOPS programmes rose and then fell in the late 1970s to early 1980s, but we do not know how many of these people actually received help with ALLN, let alone progressed within these programmes (MSC, 1978; Wallis and Elsey, 1981; ALBSU, 1981 reported that 3,500 people were enrolled in pre-TOPS programmes offering 21 hours of study weekly).

Despite basic numbers from 1985 onwards, there is little information about the different linguistic and ethnic groups who participated in ALLN programmes. A survey of ALLN by Brooks *et al* in 2001 found that around 15 per cent of learners in literacy classes had a mother-tongue language other than English. In the early 1980s, 172 separate languages were being spoken in schools in ILEA and across this time period there have been substantial changes in the composition of ethnic and linguistic minority populations (see Linguistic Minorities Project, 1985). These changes had implications for literacy and numeracy as well as for ESOL teachers. As one East London-based ESOL practitioner explained:

> the constituency of literacy classes have changed big time ... in the late 80's the literacy classes were full of white working class and Afro-Caribbeans. Ten years later they are full of 2nd generation Turkish and Bengali in that area. (HC, ESOL Practitioner, London)

ESOL learners have a very wide range of educational backgrounds, ranging from highly qualified professionals to those who have never had access to schooling or literacy in their mother tongue (see Schellekens, 2001). The situation of Afro-Caribbean students was particularly ambiguous, since patois was not recognised by many as a language in its own right:

> When I arrived in England in the 1960s it was a cultural shock to me. I thought I spoke English when I arrived but I learned I didn't. I was ridiculed and laughed at in school. Teachers said I was backward and uneducated be-cause of my accent. Everyone at school said I was speaking slang because patois wasn't a language. Very soon I started to believe that maybe everyone was right by saying patois was slang for I had never seen it written down. (Sonia Bernard, in Harris and Savitzky, 1988)

Special projects in both Manchester and London addressed the needs of Caribbean students, but the lessons from these about language variety were not mainstreamed (Morris and Nwenmele, 1994; Craven and Jackson, 1986; Schwab and Stone, 1987). Other groups also appear to have been margina-lised as provision developed. Students with disabilities and learning difficul-ties were sidelined in the effort to show ALLN learners as 'normal' people (Jones and Charnley, 1978; Banks, 1982; Clarke, 1989:18-19). A significant minority of people (see Jones and Charnley, 1978; Sanders undated; Hamilton and Stasinopolous, 1987) arrived from an education in special school where they felt they had been denied opportunities to develop. They were anxious to lose the labels that had held them back for so long. Dyslexia did become re-cognised within policy and practice (see Klein, 1993; Herrington, 2005) but ironically, the needs of students with other physical and sensory disabilities or with mental health problems were largely hidden within the mainstream practice and policy of ALLN, as in education more generally.

Profiles of individual adult learners
Student profiles have been widely used to lobby for funding and to advocate for policy, from the original *Right to Read* manifesto to the *Skills for Life* strategy document. Practitioners used them to get the attention of national

and local media. Learners' experiences are represented in complex ways that allow certain things to be emphasised and others left out. If we look at the images of the time of the literacy campaign (on the cover of the BBC handbook, for example), we find that they were mainly male, white, employed in unskilled or skilled manual craft work but there are also examples of the 'self-made manager' challenging the link between literacy and social class. Line drawings are used, rather than photographs. In documentary films, potential learners were seen as shadowy figures, fearful of exposure. As unemployment becomes a key issue, the learner becomes unemployed. Women become more prominent. By the time we reach *Skills for Life*, the majority of students are presented as being in transition from unemployment to work, progressing rapidly in their lives. There is a wider ethnic mix. People's full names are used. They face the camera confidently in the full-page photographs and are accompanied by computers.

Typical stories in the written profiles of adult learners include: motivation, aspirations and need that tells about everyday practical frustrations, barriers and instrumental tasks to be done. Another story emphasises the disorganisation of everyday experience, chaos and complexity, multiple barriers and deprivations. There is a tale about biological limitations and the effects of physical disabilities on learning. There is a heroic access story; and there is a story of 'finding yourself' as a writer (or mathematician). The change from home tuition to group work has shifted the tutor/learner relationship away from the learners' own turf to the classroom. Consequently tutors often do not know as much about the day-to-day reality of their students' lives as they did when they were home tutors (Herrington, 1994).

Autobiographical accounts

Hundreds of pieces of student writing exist (see Chapter 8). A large selection of these is held in the Changing Faces archive at Lancaster University and there are other collections around the country (see Appendix 2). There are accounts from women, from travellers, from prisoners and from ESOL learners. The writers provide information about their family backgrounds, their experiences of work and unemployment. There is information about health and disability, including mental health; about education and learning as people look back on their experiences of initial schooling and compare them with those of their own children. They offer information on their identities as learners, stories about what makes a good or a bad teacher, discipline and what makes a good learning environment, recruitment and their experiences of training and learning at/for work. There is information on lifelong learning more generally and on their learning preferences and activities in everyday life, attitudes to qualifications and assessment and their thoughts about policy issues such as paying for education (e.g. Bandali, 1976; Students at the Adult Literacy Classes at Brighton Polytechnic, 1978; Frost and Hoy, 1980; Eden Grove Women's Group,1982; Frank, 1992) .

People take part in classes through concerns about numeracy and literacy in relation to children's schooling and development; the barriers they experience in getting and progressing in work; desires to become personally more independent in everyday tasks related to literacy; access to further education; preparation for particular hurdles, like entrance tests for driving or nursing (see Charnley and Jones, 1981; Mace and Moss, 1988; Sanders, undated). Sometimes people have a long-standing sense of having missed out on education which translates into strong but quite general ambitions to improve their numeracy and literacy. They feel that important doors have been shut, that they are 'outside the long-word club' (Gardener, 1985). Sometimes such ambitions are triggered suddenly by events in their lives that make them reassess their relationship to literacy, numeracy and/or language, such as divorce, promotion or having children. In addition, there is a prevailing notion of confidence that has always been voiced by tutors and learners alike in ALLN (Mace, 1979, 59-68). This reflects the strong symbolic value of literacy and numeracy as well as its practical value in conferring status, opening access to new opportunities, its gate keeping role and use as a common yardstick to judge people's general competence and how cultured they are. In late 20th/21st century popular Western culture, literacy stands as a proxy for intelligence and education. It follows that perceived weakness in literacy shows a person to be either thick or ignorant, terms with strong emotional resonance. Paradoxically, although good numeracy skills are highly respected, it is much more socially acceptable to be poor at numbers.

The case studies presented in the Gatehouse collection as 'typical' literacy learners express some additional themes: a sense of isolation and the importance of finding others in the same situation; the skill and investment in hiding literacy difficulties because of a fear of rejection and bullying or taunting; experiences of being ignored, overlooked and pushed to one side in school, of being labelled stupid, and how to shake this off. They describe the many causes of educational underachievement including health, war and other dislocations in their lives that caused them to miss out on schooling.

Experiences of ALLN provision and preferences about formal learning

Many positive success stories told by students say that experiences of provision can be life-changing. Residential courses, in particular, are described as powerful and popular events:

> I said I'd think about coming, but thought 'no'. But I did. Thought 'No, I will hate it' But I was wrong. I've really got into it, the people are sound. It's taught me a lot. It's been wild. (Louise Pollett, July 1992, Ways of Learning Weekend)

There are also stories of continuing struggle and drop out. As Clarke comments in her study of the experiences of adults learning in Hackney in the 1980s, 'for most literacy students, the goals they leave set themselves will take many, many years to achieve' (Clarke, 1989:16). The time pressure on adults to achieve has increased dramatically in recent years and the attempt to put close limits around what counts as achievement. Brooks *et al* (2001) reviewed the statistical evidence on progress and achievement and concluded that it was minimal and inconclusive. Early studies by Jones and Charnley, 1978 and by Charnley and Jones, 1981, elaborated on the concept of success, and other small-scale studies such as Sanders (undated) and Abell, 1992 confirm that there are significant social and emotional as well as cognitive and linguistic dimensions to the learning in ALLN. Gains in confidence and self-esteem are repeatedly mentioned by tutors and students alike. Adult learners place a high value on individual attention from teachers and being treated as equals, both qualities that they felt were often lacking in their earlier experience of education. They want time to learn at their own pace, and a stable learning environment in which to study. Many are primarily interested in developing their writing and spelling rather than their reading. Their study goals are diverse, ranging from short, specific aims related to their work, to long-term, life-changing ambitions.

A special issue of a newsletter *In Our Own Words* in 1984 by the voluntary scheme Cambridge House, includes interviews with students about their experiences of learning and being involved with management of the scheme. These emphasise the importance of being careful about the naming of people and courses and the finding that 'schemes are very keen to involve students in the organising of their work, but have not really worked out how to do it effectively' (p.14). Attitudes of people outside the scheme are important and people develop various strategies of dealing with these:

> I look at it this way. I'm trying to pick up on what I lost out. You know it's no good ... you going to keep thinking about what other people saying. You'll

never get anywhere. You got to be strong. (Student, quoted in Cambridge House, 1984)

Adults have a great deal to say about their previous experiences of schooling and the reasons why they did not learn as much as they could have. This quote from one of the NCDS interviews suggests how the feeling of not being valued or expected to achieve in turn affects peoples' own identity and attitudes to learning in ways that carry on into the future. 'Barry' says of his experience of school that it was:

> horrible ... They didn't want to teach me and I didn't want to be taught ... The street I was brought up in was a notorious street and because of that as soon as you walked through them doors at that school ... you knew straight away they didn't want to know you, you didn't want to know them ... You knew they didn't want to bother with you, you just didn't bother ... we were pushed to one side. And I think it's a shame really because ... now I'm beginning to think well there's so much that's up there and I'm not stupid by any means. I just think, well all right, what if I'd have made more of an effort? But at that age you don't think that, do you? (NCDS interviewee, 'Barry')

Given their past experiences, a major emphasis for adults returning to learn is the point of contact with the service, and their efforts to get onto a course. The long process of decision-making, the expectations and the terror of the first step across the threshold are recurrent saturated messages from adult learners, well described in this quote:

> When I went to education I expected a hell of lot more time than I got. I expected every day. To make the decision to go, and to go – you can't des-cribe it – to get in that door. Then you have to tell them why you're there and you may have to repeat it three or four times ... I think the hardest part was to accept the tutors who were younger than me. I was old enough to be their father. That in itself was degrading. I couldn't go back. I had to go forward. (Joe Flanagan, in Hamilton *et al*, 1994)

Adults' accounts focus on their efforts to find out about what is on offer, or a visit to a college. Their attempts to find the right advice or suitable course come over as not just being psychologically difficult but *practically* confusing. In the few cases where people started courses, they may not run to the end of their promised time, they get interrupted or move venue, or tutors leave. It is complex to fit studying around work commitments, health problems or family commitments and transport needs. In these respects, adults' ex-periences of learning are fragmented and mirrors tutors' accounts of their working lives. There are a number of illustrations of this from the NCDS inter-views. For example, 'Colin' (P13) calls himself (as many other people do) a 'hands on learner'. His experiences of learning as an adult are all work-related: roofing, welding and plastering. The combination of changing jobs, fitting studying in with shifts and unstable provision have led to an interrupted study history:

> I've got a certificate for the brick laying one, but the plastering one they packed it in half way through doing it. I was travelling all the way to M from here to do this one-day course and then after about three weeks or maybe a month they said, 'oh we're going to pack it in. You can go brick laying if you want'. I said 'Well I don't want to do that, I've done it. I want to learn plastering'. I want to be able to do what they call a 'jobber' now, you see. You can turn your hand to doing anything. And they said, 'Well, we're packing the plastering in because we can't recycle. It just gets thrown, so it's costing too much. ('Colin' NCDS interviewee)

Later, he made a tentative approach through the *learndirect* phoneline to enrol on a computer course. When the information pack didn't arrive, he didn't pursue it any further. This is the student's-eye view of progression and drop-out, both of which measure the system's ability to meet adult learners' educational needs.

The notion of dropping out is a complex one requiring flexibility in programme definitions, since many part-time students attend irregularly and drop back in to courses at a later date, depending on the other demands in their lives (See McGivney, 2003). People drop in and out of provision in ways that are perplexing to institutional life. A small-scale ALBSU 1992-1993 survey based on seven LEAs (Kambouri and Francis, 1994) found that more than half the students enrolled in numeracy and literacy programmes left during the year, most of them during the first two or three weeks, because they felt the course was unsuitable. One-third of learners progressed to further courses or into employment. Tutors did not always know why students had left and the survey also found a significant discrepancy between teacher and student reports on reasons for leaving. A later study of ESOL learners (Kambouri, Toutounji, and Francis, 1996) found similar dropout rates from part-time classes (two to six hours per week) although the rate were halved for intensive classes (seventeen to twenty-one hours per week). The most comprehensive figures about progression and drop-out rates come from an FEFC inspection report in 1998. This covers ALLN students enrolled in further education colleges in England and estimates that 81 per cent of ALLN students stay to the end of the course, and of these, 60 per cent achieve the qualifications or learning goals they were aiming for (FEFC, 1998).

Everyday literacies and informal learning

It is important to look at the ways in which peoples' everyday lives work around limited ways of using literacy and numeracy, the issues that take precedence when they make decisions and the support systems they draw on. Evidence from the New Literacy Studies that has grown over the last 15 years (see Chapter 2) offers detailed accounts of how literacy and numeracy fit into the ecology of people's lives, the informal support and learning activities that surround them, and how they are embedded in the multiple issues and priorities of everyday living.

This research evidence has accumulated, both through qualitative studies and successive analyses of longitudinal cohort data (Barton, 1994; Barton and Hamilton, 1998; Hamilton, 2005; Hamilton and Stasinopoulos, 1987; Bynner and Parsons 1998). This evidence suggests that a great deal of informal learning occurs. Support for literacy is offered within the relationships of family, neighbourhood and community. People with limited technical skills in literacy and numeracy are not necessarily marginalised or excluded in their everyday lives and they are often able to keep one step ahead in addressing their literacy and numeracy needs. Themes emerging from our interviews with the NCDS adults confirm these earlier studies and we illustrate these briefly below. Our evidence helps to explain why many who report such limited skills do not seek to participate in formal learning and why there is a difference between self-reported and externally assessed difficulties with basic skills.

> I get a new appliance and I'm using it and he says have you read the manual? No. Are you going to? Well it's working. And he will sit ... I mean when we got the TV ... he will sit there and 'oh it does this, it does that'. But he has to have all the clocks set. Probably if he wasn't here learning it I would do it, I would find out how to set the clock. I would have to read the book ... INT So since he is around you don't have to? RES Why keep a dog and bark yourself? ('Joy' NCDS interviewee)

Such uses of 'scribes' (see Mace, 2002), brokers, mediators and advocates for literacy and numeracy are ubiquitous in the data from research studies. The specific roles of these brokers vary across settings and participants (whether in the home, prison or workplace). The same person can be novice at one moment, expert the next, with a change of situation or topic. Expertise and support are offered within reciprocal relationships, exchanges of skills and services. Particularly useful brokers are those who can mediate between the local, everyday, informal world and the world of official institutional literacies.

> I am the money person. If anyone came on the phone and asks anything to do with money or things then I do it. He isn't thick by no means but he doesn't really want the worry of it.
>
> INT And that's one of your jobs?
>
> RES Yes and that doesn't bother me, I like doing it really.
>
> INT Do people come to you for advice?
>
> RES Yes sometimes yes. I suppose they do really yes. My friend has been having a bit ... she thought someone was being funny to her at work but I hadn't really noticed and she asked me what I thought she should do ... a lot of people do talk to me like that yes, funnily enough. Probably because I sort of listen and see both sides of things ('Sandra' NCDS interviewee)

Adults describe a large amount of intergenerational learning especially around new technologies and new languages. Changing contexts, history, cultural change and dislocation affect peoples' abilities to demonstrate their skilfulness. Adults learn from children. Children learn from grandparents, their friends and siblings. The fluidity of relationships supports different authority relations, and hence different identities. Individuals retain autonomy and control over how far, how fast or whether at all to learn. The evidence about scribes and brokers leads to idea of networks and the importance of social capital is certainly borne out in this data (Field, 2005).

> C, the little 8 year old fella, he comes and we'll write words with him, and he'll say 'Can you spell this for me?', and I'll go 'Auntie J can't spell, go and see your Uncle R'. So he goes over to R and R'll do that, and he'll come back and he'll go 'But you can do the maths, you do my sums, you do my sums', and I'll do sums for him. ('Eva' NCDS interviewee)
>
> INT OK what about mobile phones ... do you text message?
>
> RES I do yeah, now me daughter's taught me how to do it! [laugh]. She said to me, we went to H____ on Bank Holiday Monday and on the way back I got a text and I was trying to send one back and she said, 'mother are you writing a four page letter?' [laugh] Because it was taking me that long she said, 'give it to me what do you want to say?' [laugh] Oh dear. ('Pam' NCDS interviewee)

Examples of everyday assessment (dog shows, poetry 'slams' ie competitions, vegetable competitions, fell runs and talent contests) show that 'what counts' as success is locally defined within a specific community of practice. These yardsticks of personal efficacy in everyday life are more subtle and multifaceted than educational assessments, embedded in social relationships, complementary abilities and personal.

> I would not go to college to learn, to do business studies or to do my own books. The way I think is: well no I don't want to do that, I know I probably wouldn't be able to do that so ... like I have an accountant and it would be just like 'there you are, that is your job, you are good with figures you sort that out, I'll decorate your front room' you know ... Something that I know I can do. I'd only do something that I know I could do. ('Graham' NCDS interviewee)

Everyday language, literacy and numeracy learning offer physical immersion in the targeted activity, opportunities for hands on participation and practice. It uses all the senses. Everyday learning is do-it-yourself. It scavenges available resources and expertise, appropriating these to new ends. It is 'making do', 'bodging', 'getting by', and 'just doing it'. All these phrases are used repeatedly in the NCDS interviews with adults, as in this example of unconventional learning within the dynamics of family life:

> I ... bought flat packs and built it all and then fitted all the worktops, took out the whole for the sink, fitted the sink, plumbed it all in ... My dad had come over and said right that's the hot pipe and put an H on it and that's the cold pipe, and when you put your taps on you do this and do this. So he told me what to do. I am a bodger. I was the middle of three girls and if ever there was an argument between mum and dad, dad would storm off to the garage, and it was 'G go and sort your father out' ... there are pictures of me as a child up to my knees in oil in the engine. I helped him take the engine out of one our cars and put it in, it's nothing to me changing the exhaust on a car or putting new shocks in, things like that. And then my brother-in-law got a garage and I used to go down there at a weekend and grind the valves in. ('Gillie' NCDS interviewee)

A final, far-reaching point is that everyday literacy learning does not respect boundaries between different communication media. It uses oral or written language, images, equations, symbols, sound, music, gestures, graphs, artefacts. Phone, screen, print and face-to-face interactions are used in combination and interchangeably, dependent on the task, convenience of access and preferred learning styles. This has led writers such as Kress (2003) and Gee (2004) to talk about 'semiotic landscapes' or domains that are used to communicate distinctive types of meanings. Everyday learning operates with activities and meanings created in a multi-modal space and resists attempts to categorise by particular types of technology.

> I mean on certain things like when I got the washing machine and dish washer yes I read the manuals but only as far as I needed to know. I don't read them cover to cover. I just switch it on, right I do that button, that button, this light comes up. Or if the light comes up I will get the book out, oh red light that's what it means. ('Jan' NCDS interviewee)

Taken together, the evidence we have pieced together gives some clear answers to the question of why people do not participate in ALLN. Firstly, everyday uses and practices of literacy and numeracy are part of the informal and often unrecognised learning that goes on within family, community and workplace. Through these informal practices people 'just do it', they 'get by' and get 'settled', supporting and exchanging skills and expertise, fashioning their practical lives and sense of identity within the limits they perceive for themselves. Brokers, mentors in the family, neighbourhood and workplace can be especially important in this process.

Many aspects of literacy and numeracy can seem either irrelevant (particularly in routine employment) or so embedded in everyday activities that people are not aware of them as such. Any difficulties or limitations they experience are attributed to other things. In the case, for example, where limited literacy or numeracy is associated with a complex range of other factors, such as health or long-term disability, this presents much more salient constraints on people, including key limitations on their employment opportunities and their ability to participate regularly in educational activities.

Finally people's identities are invested in their experiences of education and their management of these. Points of learning (Barton *et al*, 2006) are often moments of tension and change and they support changing identities as well as technical skills (see Fingeret and Drennon, 1997). Our NCDS interviews show that in later life people reach a working compromise between their ambitions and their actual lives. They have developed support systems and also deep identities built around the experience of exclusion. Being asked to challenge that settlement may be seen as threatening and too risky, given past experiences of education. At 44 years of age, some NCDS members felt they were 'too old to learn now' and their attention had shifted to their children's success in education.

What do we know about learners' perspectives on policy?

Learners' experiences of provision have reflected what is going on in policy. They report chaotic, disrupted and fragmented access. They mirror practitioners' comments about funding and staffing constraints even though they don't talk about these in terms of policy as such. It was quite a shock to discover how hard to reach the provision could be for learners and what people have had to deal with in terms of lack of support and scant order and continuity in their learning. We wonder how far this may have been true of their experience at school as well, especially those in special education or schools that struggled to retain teachers and used supply staff on a regular basis.

What evidence do we have that students ever tried to affect this situation and to shape policy? At what points and in what ways could they be seen as policy actors? There were some organisations and networks that were organised by students and others had significant input into decision-making through management committees, making choices about literacy work, confronting issues about racism and lack of funding. Thus the National Students Association, the *Write First Time* newspaper collective, the Federation of Worker Writers and Publishers (FWWCP), and Pecket Well College in Halifax were all learner-run. Other democratically run organisations included the Lee Centre in Lewisham, the Book Place in Peckham, the Brent (London) and Evington Road (Leicester) Open Learning Centres. Although trade unions have been involved in particular basic skills projects over the years (Bonnerjea, 1987) especially in public sector workplaces, there has been very little serious advocacy from the organised labour movement for the right to a basic education in general. Trades union influence itself has declined over this period and, whilst union learning representatives now operate in a wide range of workplaces, the demand for statutory day release or time off to learn has all but disappeared from the political agenda.

There is little evidence that students complain about the quality of the premises that they learn in, though they have certainly remarked on this in passing. As Jones and Charnley (1978:87) note, 'the teacher filled the whole of their vision and they rarely mentioned teaching methods or materials'. Many were accepting rather than judgemental and, as one person put it: 'you don't like to grumble when you are getting something for free' (Sanders, undated, p.14).

Issues and debates emerging across the whole period
Since the 1970s, public attitudes and perceptions of ALLN learners have changed substantially and with these changes have come different languages to describe them, language that is still not settled today. Perceptions moved from seeing adults as illiterate, shamed and hidden, and in need of temporary remedial help, to a more informed and nuanced understanding of adults' needs and aspirations around language and numeracy, and awareness that a permanent lifelong learning infrastructure is needed to keep pace with the changing demands of adult life, especially in relation to cultural displacement of populations, employment and new communication technologies. The initial focus on responding to adults who came forward was widened to an interest in and concern for widening participation among those who did not take part in learning. The national agencies made extensive use of national and international research to document who these people were and

define them as targets. The media still use old stereotypes from time to time, and views of ESOL learners are still riven with tensions and prejudices that accompany their status as asylum seekers, refugees and migrant workers.

To what extent have adult students been agents for change in the field? Current policy discourse presents many of them as reluctant to learn and a growing body of research has shown the extent of informal learning and support that people rely on to get by, without the help of formal lifelong learning. Though self-organised learning for literacy and numeracy, and trade union involvement, have been persistent features of the field, these have never been the main driving forces for development. This has been much more top-down, first by voluntary agencies, some local authorities and the media, and more recently by national government.

Once enrolled in provision, however, students have been frequently involved in advocating for funding and have allowed their testimonies to be used to promote policy and to avoid funding cuts. Token students have appeared on decision-making bodies including the Moser Committee. In a few programmes they have become involved with local management or have become student representatives or involved with wider networks, but this has not been the norm. The short-lived National Students Association indicates the general lack of direct involvement in decision-making that most learners have had, the token ways in which students are included (if at all) in consultations and the little-expressed need for more involvement from the student body itself.

It is not clear that the messages from student-published accounts have been taken seriously by either practice or policy. These messages are: adults place a high value on individual attention from teachers and respectful relationships that can help rebuild the confidence lost through past experiences of failure, bullying and ridicule. Whilst policy and assessment focus on *reading*, adults repeatedly emphasise importance of developing their *writing*. Social attitudes sustain the notion of the problem of illiteracy. It is not just a matter of skills. The attitudes and behaviour of others enforce the symbolic value of literacy and numeracy and the feelings of social exclusion of people who have under achieved. Adult learners are aware that a lifetime of educational failure cannot be solved in a few weeks and consequently need sustained and stable opportunities to study, possibly over a long period of time. People can keep one jump ahead in a textually mediated world, using the resources and support available in everyday environments nimbly and creatively. This means that while formal education can be life-changing, for the vast majority of adults it is just one, imperfect resource among others to support the development of literacy, numeracy and communication.

Tensions around learners include the need to make them visible in order to maintain funding but not to present deficit images. Continual changes in the naming of the field, the programmes and participants, indicate that this tension is alive and unresolved. There are also tensions between the evident diversity of adult learners and the needs for standardisation; between the desire of funders to see quick results and the needs of learners for longer-term study. The increasing need to show results in ALLN programmes has led to more opportunities for confident and higher-level students who can be moved quickly through courses, at the expense of those with more complex, long-term needs and goals.

As the political climate has changed, the way in which adults are represented as having rights or obligations to learn has changed, with an increasingly punitive approach to marginal groups, who have come to be seen as having a *duty as a citizen* to improve their skills (whether ESOL, literacy or numeracy). A strong, expert voice has emerged from the evidence based policy that is defining for adult learners what their needs and strategies should be for entering the mainstream of society through education. Who defines need and the power dynamics in relationships between student, tutor and policy has been in balance since the beginning of the 1970s and is revisited in later chapters as we look at self versus external definitions of curriculum, goals and assessment.

At its best, ALLN has attracted a different group of adults into lifelong learning and has been an important part of the access movement. It has helped improve practices in recruitment, and argued for local provision to be organised more flexibly. The evidence on informal learning, networks of support and resources in the community are much less well understood in professional lifelong learning circles. This chapter has assembled many insights from the perspective of the adults who might benefit from ALLN. It is clear, though, that the diversity of both adult learners and the provision that has developed makes it unlikely that we will find a neat and compact way of characterising their experience.

5

The practitioners

I mean God knows that in those days they took me on and I hadn't got any training at all except for a few weeks of experience as a literacy volunteer. I think I had an introductory week course or something that you used to get in those days. So I mean looking back I think it was really shocking. (JW, Manchester)

First of all I went as a volunteer tutor because I had got young children, which was a home tutor, and I later on became a class tutor and then went on to become an assistant organiser. So that was roughly over ten years really, while the children were growing up. (JC, Leics)

Very few men want to come in and are happy to work for the part-time hours that we had to offer, so the people who came in tended to be women who took on that work ... you've only got to go to any conference of ESOL and you know it's 90 per cent female. (JJ and CC, Manchester)

We can locate the experiences of practitioners in a much wider debate about agency and conflict. Avis *et al*, (1996, 2002) examined the way in which the current government has viewed education as key to economic prosperity. Through the policies and reports that have emanated since 1997, including the Kennedy Report *Learning Works: Widening Participation in Further Education* (1997), *The Learning Age* (DfEE, 1998), *Learning to Succeed* (1999), along with Moser (1999) and the creation of the Further Education National Training Organisation (FENTO) standards (1999) for teaching and learning in further education, there has been a commodification of the tutor, and an accompanying loss of control and intensification of work. Although we concentrated on the three decades until 2000, our practitioners have faced changes to their employment practices as a result of these initiatives, along with their colleagues across the Learning and Skills Sector. Indeed, the elements identified by Avis *et al* which result from the managerialism and marketisation of FE (Avis, 2001: 64) are applicable to basic skills. These include loss of control, intensification of labour, increase in administration, perceived marginalisation of teaching and stress on measurable performance indicators. Practitioners were strategically compliant with such measures, in other words, reconciling themselves to initiatives through 'artful pragmatism' (Gleeson and Shain, 1999:482).

The early years

The term 'practitioner' covers a range of roles. People might be involved in ALLN as volunteers working with an individual learner or a group. They could be hourly paid tutors, outreach workers, full-time or fractional lecturers in adult and community learning, further education colleges, voluntary organisations and work-based learning provision. They work as managers and organisers, and even as directors of organisations, private, statutory and voluntary, which may not even have basic skills as their primary function.

Our research has uncovered deep-seated characteristics that provide some cohesion to what is at first glance a very disparate field. This chapter draws upon the interviews we conducted with practitioners, supported by documentary analysis.

The workforce has been, from the early 1970s, overwhelming female and hourly paid if teaching, Even volunteers tend to be female, and have been since the original campaign in 1975, where 82 per cent of those who responded to the *On the Move* programme were women (Jones and Charnley, 1978). Today there is a large, national infrastructure which employs full-time, fractional and hourly paid staff in further education colleges, adult community programmes, and work-based learning programmes as well as in voluntary organisations and in the workplace. To see how this developed during the past thirty years, any ALBSU annual report provides a snapshot of the basic skills workforce at the time and how it was supported.

The annual reports even show the number of hours worked by part-time staff, and of those, nearly 50 per cent taught only two hours per week. The interesting omission in the report is a breakdown of staff by sex! By 1998, the FEFC report on adult basic skills did not even include figures of staff employed, although it acknowledged that there were many employed on a part-time basis, although BSA sources could at least identify the percentage of provision in further and adult education (Hamilton and Merrifield, 1999).

Table 5.1 Literacy and numeracy staff in the first decade since _On the Move_

Date	Staff	FT	PT	Volunteers
1976	3161	80	3081	38,310
1986	9000	900	8100	20,000
1996	12,900	1290	11,610	13,400

In 1986, 1,500 training opportunities were provided by ALBSU through its regional programmes.

Table 5.2 Training opportunities in 1986

Initial Training	Inservice Training
9000 (volunteers)	7000 (volunteers) 4000 (tutors)

In 1986, ESOL had been included in the annual report for the first time.

Table 5.3 ESOL staff employed in 1986

Date	Staff	FT	PT	Volunteers
1986	2,500	14%	86%	4500

Practitioners held a variety of qualifications and had extensive previous knowledge in a range of fields. ESOL practitioners often, but not exclusively, held qualifications and experience in languages. Literacy tutors were just as highly qualified but not specifically in literacy. Numeracy tutors ranged from those who were maths specialists to those who had few formal qualifications in maths or numeracy. The latter group often taught the subject simply because their organiser needed to teach a numeracy class and approached literacy tutors to do so. There was overlap between dealing with functional literacy and numeracy, for example in using bus timetables, just as there was overlap between literacy, numeracy and language. ESOL tutors we interviewed thought literacy tutors were less qualified and less knowledgeable than themselves about the more technical aspects of teaching literacy. The hegemony of literacy, though, as the basic skill most cited and known by the general public and politicians, is acknowledged by all three groups.

Many of the people we interviewed are still in the field, even if they have moved from being hourly paid tutors to managers and, in some cases, directors of national agencies. Although they represent a disparate field, they are united in their enthusiasm, energy and excitement. Their stories are a powerful dedication to the learner, to their colleagues and to the field.

> And we were all on a crusade really, we did see ourselves as doing something very important and so useful. (AZ, London)

Despite constant changes to their working conditions, they continue to fight, duck and weave, whilst maintaining a sound sense of humour and irony.

> And we've managed, you know, like little resistant fighters, to keep going for a long time. (JB, Manchester)

What did practitioners say that enabled us to reach these conclusions?

Entry stories

We identified a number of pathways into basic skills work. In the early 1970s, when the field was new, people came forward, both as volunteers and then as part-time tutors, with backgrounds in primary school teaching, special needs work, foreign language teaching and, to a lesser extent, involvement in civic or social action. Tutors who began as volunteers were offered work almost immediately in ways that today would not meet equal opportunities policies for recruitment and selection. There were two main reasons for becoming involved; deciding to volunteer through a commitment to social action, or returning to work part-time due to family commitments. The majority of people we interviewed joined because they had previous experience of teaching and the conditions of hourly-paid work enabled them to combine their role as parents and teachers.

> Standard route of any woman with children, by then I had children, met somebody waiting in the nursery queue who said 'we need an adult numeracy tutor'. I said 'oh well I teach that'. (PH, London)

The other major factor which underpinned so many practitioners' decisions to become involved in the field was through a sense of political or social justice. It is likely that this is not a sufficient condition, but a necessary one, combined with the fundamental need to earn a living!

> It's political and it's a social conscience. I think a lot of people who go into this work are like that. Not everybody of course. For some people it's a job, its teaching and that's all right isn't it. But I think there are a lot of people who have quite a heightened social conscience. (JC Leics)

As well as FE and AE, a range of private training providers with government funding to work with unemployed adults also developed basic skills provision. Our respondents (who were mainly based in AE and FE) were critical of these organisations and the tutors working in them, partly because staff were taken on with minimal qualifications, and given poor conditions of service whilst the organisations were primarily profit-making. Prison educators and those who worked in the workplace but were funded through college or voluntary provision or were employed by the organisation Workbase were not subject to the same criticisms. This indicates something of the values and ideology of 'good practice' in the field.

Volunteers

The number of volunteers involved in basic skills reached a peak of 45,000 in the mid-1970s falling to 20,000 by the mid-1980s (ALBSU, 1987). Volunteers, like tutors, joined for a number of reasons and many moved into paid work as a result. Should volunteers be used at all? Arguments for the deployment of volunteers related to the notion that it was time to break the mould of education practices, particularly as adults with literacy problems had not fared well using traditional educational means. Drawing upon people from a wide range of backgrounds would ensure that the adult learners were given support in ways that might not have been possible through traditional teaching techniques. However, there were powerful arguments against using volunteers, seen as exploitation when there should be a government commitment with appropriate funding for paid staff.

> It's easy for them sometimes to appear to be patronising. But generally they were good hearted people who really wanted to help. (AP, volunteer at Cambridge House, London)

Volunteers were viewed by organisers as both a 'blessing and a curse' and over time they fell out of favour as provision moved towards small group work in centres. Group work was considered better for the students, ensuring consistency and enabling students to share their experiences. The move to paid tutoring, though, was affected by concerns about quality and also concern about not wanting to criticise people who had devoted time and effort to help out in the field. Volunteers were still used in groups, but in smaller numbers than when involved in one-to-one tutoring. Although many of our interviewees had been volunteers, contradictory views of volunteers ranging from supportive to disparaging were expressed during the interviews, seen from a managerial perspective.

> I was appalled at the actual non-existence of real knowledge in practitioners who were out there delivering basic skills. You know it was a cottage industry with volunteers put into teaching. And lovely as they were they didn't know how to teach. (FL, London)

Yet volunteers were responsible for the early successes of the adult literacy movement, and their ability to contribute, not only in teaching on an individual basis, through meeting learners in their own homes, but in helping an adult literacy centre become the welcoming and enjoyable venue for so many adult learners. Early after the BBC campaign, the success of recruiting potential volunteers was noted by the *On the Move* producer David Hargreaves (1980).

> We now know, and urge other broadcasters to consider, the degree to which public sympathy and concern can be channelled into positive volunteer effort, which is altruistic and motivated by compassion and simple 'goodwill'. ... this is perhaps the greatest, and the least tapped [potential] in the world of education. (Hargreaves, 1980:148)

Whether volunteers were deployed as fully as they might have been remains untested.

Gift time

Throughout our interviews of people involved in the 1970s and early 1980s, practitioners told stories of enjoying the participation in staff development events, resource and materials production, and student writing events. This was often undertaken with no pay, and usually in the evenings and at weekends.

> Tutors put in a hell of a lot of time, unpaid. We organised for ourselves Saturday morning training sessions to get together ... I don't remember that anybody ever got paid for going on them. We just went because we were very keen and we wanted to find things out and develop our teaching. (JG, London)

This 'gift time' became a source of discontent when the context in which people worked was threatened. People are happy to give up evenings and weekends when they feel valued, but become angry when they are subject to re-organisation, inspection or threatened by redundancy, yet continue their 'gift time' for the sake of learners and peers.

Developing careers?

Not everyone developed careers by moving from voluntary work to part-time teaching and on to organising, management and national policymaking, although we did interview key figures who had forged careers in precisely this way. Women *were* in senior management roles, as organisers and managers. Yet the workforce often suffered from a lack of status despite the professionalism of such work. Practitioners joked about the lack of career structure and generous pay. Their disenfranchisement shows as they talk about their work, and in inspection reports which find poorer quality of teaching attributed to the casualisation of the further education sector in particular (see ALBSU annual reports for numbers of paid full and part-time staff, FEFC 1998, Appendix 5 for statistics on part-time staff in the FEFC/LSC sector in Hillier and Jameson, 2004, Avis *et al*, 2002).

> Our rate of pay was so abysmally low and still is very low ... whatever we try and do we get beaten back because of the rate of pay. (MH, Leics)

ALBSU was aware that the way to improve the quality of the learning experience for students was to improve the pay and conditions of organisers who were responsible for professional development.

> Too often part-time organisers paid for no more than a few hours per week are expected to undertake a volume of work that would stretch a full-time paid organiser. The choice for many women taking up a career ... is to move out of basic education to further their careers or remain and accept low status, low pay and considerable exploitation of good will. (ALBSU, 1986:2)

Funding permeates provision, and practitioners were deeply affected by funding decisions. During the 1980s and 1990s, when there were LEA cuts and reorganisation through the FHE Act, people were often redeployed, required to re-apply for their existing jobs or made redundant. On the other hand, practitioners benefited from new funding sources with new forms of provision, such as open learning, as funding streams became available. The role of the organiser was critical in garnering support to challenge cuts, establishing new opportunities and tapping into alternative funding streams, and making their presence known amongst LEA council members, FE senior management and voluntary organisation management committees. We have examples from all the case study areas of organisers launching campaigns to protect reduction or closures of programmes.

> I did get frustrated about being the poor relation and being excluded from things. And feeling almost as if you had to apologise every time you spoke to anyone about who you were and where you were from. (SH, Leics)

> So you'd just approach anybody and you'd write to get grants for things and you were just scrounging for money all the while. (JB, Leics)

Working with quality
In the 1970s, LEA courses were covered by Her Majesty's Inspectorate (HMI) and responsibility for quality rested with individual LEAs and providers but this was not a very tightly controlled or customised system. During the 1980s,

as public services came under increasing scrutiny for their cost effectiveness, professionals felt that they were not trusted to be responsible for the quality of their provision. Concern about quality was influenced by government questions about the outcomes from ten years of funding. This approach was a foundation for the later development of the Quality Mark by ALBSU, later BSA, characterised by a view of entitlement of the learner, eg, to a minimum number of hours' tuition, an initial interview, means of identifying progress and a professional development strategy for the staff. Most LEAs were claiming that their programmes were of good quality yet ALBSU field consultants sometimes saw some 'really, really awful things'.

> Certainly our quality stuff came from looking at programmes and getting concerned about them, ... in particular pretty well anyone could turn up and volunteer and teach, didn't need any qualifications at all. What went on in the classes? ... We became more unpopular after that. (AW, London).

Today, all public service must demonstrate its alignment against certain criteria, particularly Public Service Agreements (PSAs), but in the 1970s and 1980s, there was no such requirement.

Lobbying for change: pressure groups, practitioner bodies

Practitioners in ALLN developed very little national presence or organised representation. The voluntary ethos, the part-time nature of employment, the dispersal of staff in many different contexts and with different employers, terms and conditions was not conducive to organised action and networking. The voluntary sector was better organised and vocal in the early period, documenting their achievements, advocating for funding and working collaboratively with learners to voice their concerns through the National Federation of Voluntary Literacy Schemes (NFVLS). Active centres include the Friends' Centre in Brighton, Centerprise, Blackfriars, the Lee Centre in London and the Liverpool WEA Second Chance to Learn.

There are examples of local political activism in all of our case site areas. Activity typically was around protecting funding for programmes, rather than pay and conditions. We have uncovered few examples of people actively working politically within statutory organisations. The Manchester Adult Literacy Education Coalition (MALEC) was an early example of practitioners and learners together taking on the FE establishment to challenge the low status and lack of funding of adult literacy. Interestingly, both of these examples resulted in catastrophic defeat and dispersal of the people involved.

In the 1980s, the National Association for Teachers in Further and Higher Education, (NATFHE), the main trade union representing teachers in the post-compulsory sector, had an Adult Basic Education Sub-Section (ABESS) but this did not survive into the incorporation era. The ABESS newsletter from Summer 1992 shows practitioners discussing their uncertainties and concerns about the impact of incorporation on the field, debating the value of being in or out of FE, arguing that quality ALLN is possible within the business-oriented Training and Enterprise Councils (TECs), engaging in debates in the press and with politicians in national government, and reporting on parallel issues from Australia.

Only ESOL had a professional organisation, National Association for Teachers in English and Community Language, (NATECLA, originally NATESLA), which advocated on behalf of the field and contributed to policy, training, research and curriculum, through its journal *Language Issues* and circulated materials. NATECLA was instrumental in getting a separate core curriculum defined for ESOL within *Skills for Life*. Research-oriented membership organisations, such as RaPAL focused closely on links between research and practice, publishing a regular journal, whilst Adults Learning Maths (ALM) developed a stronger international base and an annual conference. Both organisations contributed to networking and to the underlying discourse through their publishing.

Strong local networks as in Manchester's Central Area Basic Skills Unit (CABSU) existed in many LEAs and counties and were often the source of long-term professional and personal links. At their best they offered support, exchange of ideas, advice, resources and professional development at times of restructuring, when people were forced to compete with one another for diminished local resources.

Professional development, training and accreditation of practitioners

Training has been an integral part of practice in ALLN. Volunteers were offered training when they joined a scheme. Initially, this professional development relied on a small cadre of volunteer organisers creating short training programmes. The BAS Volunteer Tutor Pack provided support for this work (BAS, 1976). The language experience approach required working with learners on areas of their interest, rather than using inappropriate children's resources. Indeed, much of the training focused on materials development in the early years, simply because there was a dearth of appropriate material for adult learners. The practical focus of the training can still be seen in professional development programmes today.

The amount of training varied across the country. In Norfolk, for example, much of the training took place in liaison with the East Anglia Regional Advisory Council (EARAC) in the early days. As the LEA service was expanded and more organisers were employed, so the training was structured to help professionalise the service. People in other metropolitan areas were supported well, as our Manchester case study revealed. London was complex with its different boroughs. Outer London boroughs were similar to other metropolitan and county authorities, with responsibility for education. Inner London boroughs were covered by one authority, ILEA, where training for adult educators across London in adult and further education was well supported and seen by our interviewees to be groundbreaking in its attention to issues of race and gender. The other major source of training was through ALBSU which ran regional training events, organised by practitioners and organisers. Volunteers were encouraged to attend, and indeed, there were half-day events aimed specifically at volunteers.

Practitioners drew heavily upon their networks for support. These networks operated at local, regional and national levels. ALBSU provided support through its newsletters nationally, and through regional networks with funding to meet agreed training needs, usually organised by convenors. The organisers might draw upon part-time tutors and, in some cases, volunteers and learners to provide workshops, usually on Saturdays, so that part-time tutors could attend. Nearly all the practitioners who had been involved in basic skills in the 1980s spoke favourably of the training, as it enabled them to identify their own needs and share good practice. However, ALBSU withdrew its funding for regional development in 1991, due partly to its concerns about quality. This was a deeply unpopular decision, and organisers and practitioners mentioned this specifically when discussing how they participated in professional development.

> But we used to have these training days where you would come in on a Saturday and you would learn from practitioners particular things and they were brilliant. I remember having a conversation with someone from the BSA and he just said they were a complete waste of time, nobody learnt anything, and I had a real argument with him and said actually we valued them very highly and we did learn an awful lot. But when you have that sort of attitude, which I thought was just completely stupid and totally unhelpful, and also rubbished everything that we had valued ... you know because we used to go without pay, you used to go on a Saturday and just go to learn so that you could do your job better. (JW, London)

In its last year, 1991, there were 2015 people who had been involved in regional training.

Another source of networking was the system of verifiers and moderators that developed through the 1990s, particularly those working with the Open College and with awarding bodies like City and Guilds. These networks provided a collegial space for professional discussion during the era of divisive competition during incorporation.

Professional development was increasingly important by the late 1980s, as noted by our practitioners and through analysis of documentation such as ALBSU newsletters. Yet in1986, 38 per cent of LEAs provided no initial training for paid staff, and ALBSU claimed that 51 per cent of its total grant of £2.2million was spent on Local and Special Development Projects, along with its support for regional training. By the end of the decade, funding was set aside by LEAs to train teachers. This Grant for Education to Support Teachers (GEST), funded specified aims agreed within an individual LEA, and adult education centres were able to access these providing they offered training which worked towards the aims.

With the increasing credentialisation of programmes of learning throughout the 1980s and 1990s (Gray and Griffin, 2000), professional development for basic skills practitioners followed the same route. There were generic awards, such as the City and Guilds Certificate in Further and Adult Education (the 730) which could lead to a Certificate in Education (Cert Ed). Specific awards in basic skills included the Royal Society of Arts (RSA) Diploma in Teaching and Learning in Adult Basic Education, which began in the mid-1970s with ILEA's support, and a Diploma in the Teaching of ESL. With the exception of the 730, these awards were not widely available, and particularly not funded for hourly paid staff, although in ILEA there was good support for a certificate level award, ALLAT, and the RSA Diplomas. Perhaps the most controversial but widely-used qualification was created by ALBSU in 1989, The Initial Teaching Certificate in Adult Basic Skills ((ITC), initially the 9282/3/4 but later known as the 9281. The initiative began through a mapping of volunteer training and collection of materials for a training pack which became the basis for the new qualification. City and Guilds, with its established portfolio of teaching qualifications for further education, agreed to develop what became the ITC. In 1991, City and Guilds only awarded 40 certificates, but during 2000, 6,565 people gained the award (unpublished data, City and Guilds).

There were heated debates amongst organisers who ran the scheme, and with the assessors (now known as external verifiers) about how the award was used. The limited number of hours was too brief to cover the necessary information to begin teaching basic skills. In particular, there was concern that organisations were using the award to develop their paid staff, and employing new staff with the qualification to teach groups, when the original design was only meant to equip volunteers to work with individual students.

> The 9282 City and Guilds was a wonderful course which allowed people to get into basic skills teaching but of course it shouldn't have been allowed without some other control. (MB,London)

One of the problems with the ITC was that the certificate was predicated on teaching one-to-one, whereas in ESOL provision, teaching was almost wholly undertaken with groups. ESOL tutors found it difficult to relate their assignments to the one-to-one focus. Numeracy trainers, too, were concerned that the assessed activities were not always suited to their context.

To add to the confusion at this time, an additional qualification was developed, which became known as the 9285, which had benefited from the competence-based movement and creation of national vocational qualifications (NVQs) for a more structured, outcomes-based award. The evaluation of the pilot of the award claimed that ALBSU had been 'ahead of its time' in choosing a competence-based accreditation scheme as at the time (1989-1991), NCVQ had not yet fully established its procedures, or the lead body in education. In fact, this was never established (see Naomi Sargant's evaluation report, ALBSU, 1991:17).

Our interviewees had many reservations about this award. The need to find examples of practice that could match the performance criteria and range statements of the competences was tedious and frustrating, especially as it documented existing knowledge rather than fostering new knowledge, which very experienced practitioners found traumatic.

> The 9285 is what drove me out of basic skills in the end ... I saw all the developments they [ALBSU] were making as part of moving themselves into a more controlling position with Quality Mark and training things. But again if the training things had been inspiring or at the right level then they would have had the whole field there ... I mean people used to weep doing the 9285. Grown women wept! (MH, Leics)

Even with an accreditation framework in place, many tutors were employed without any qualification to teach basic skills, something ALBSU reports noted annually, and which, even today, the current government strategy is attempting to address.

Quality Mark

ALBSU/BSA introduced its Quality Mark in 1992. It specified minimum standards for provision and aimed to enshrine aspects of good practice (e.g. student/teacher ratios) that had developed in practice over time but might not be respected by colleges or private training providers. Alan Wells, its Director defended the use of the Quality Mark by noting that a system needed to say what was 'good and bad', and which would 'drive up standards'. How was this perceived in the field?

> Certainly in '92 we went for the Q mark and where I worked was the first centre to get the Q mark. It was good in one way and it made you look at what you were doing. But it did shove you down a certain tunnel. (JW, Manchester)

> I think when the quality mark first came in, that was a sort of unifying force really, where we all were aware that we were working to standards which were externally set. (JW, London)

The Quality Mark provided organisers with an opportunity to increase resources for their provision, in order to meet the criteria defined by ALBSU and later by the BSA. There was a check list on effectiveness and organisers could use this to argue for resources from their head of service.

> Once he was hooked on the idea of us getting the quality mark, it gave me great sort of armour to say well we need this and we need that and I milked it for all it was worth! But we were the first provider in the North West to get the quality mark. (NS, Manchester)

After incorporation, the FEFC created its own inspection regime, adding further quality assurance requirements. When the LSC was created, two inspectorates, Ofsted for schools and colleges and the Adult Learning Inspectorate (ALI) would inspect the *Skills for Life* strategy amongst other FE provision. To help consistency, a *common inspection framework* was agreed. At this point the BSA's Quality Mark was abolished.

Although people who prepared for the FEFC inspection (and currently for Ofsted and ALI inspections) devoted enormous time and energy to provide evidence of the quality of their provision, they expressed positive comments about the value of inspections. Inspections help to reinforce organisers' and managers' feelings of self-worth, particularly as they affirm the good practice that they have striven for.

> I have always felt that inspections are quite useful for getting your house in order and doing all the things that you have put off. So I have always been

> fairly positive about somebody coming out and looking at the centre at the whole. (CW, Leics)

> I think all those things, the quality assurance systems, the monitoring systems, quality systems, national curriculum are really, really needed. I think they are needed to ensure that people get a minimum good delivery. (SC, Norfolk)

But it is not always appreciated:

> If you were told you were great then you would just breathe a sigh of relief. And if you were told that you were not so great then what do you do? You know it's very miserable. (AZ, London)

We can see, then, that practitioners have been influenced by many issues over the past thirty years. They have had to help develop the field into being, and then see it being subject to scrutiny which has not always been aligned to the vision of the participants. They have used networks to help each other find how to work effectively with their learners, they have taken action where provision has been under threat, and they have undertaken professional development, often unpaid, to help ensure that they keep abreast of the changing nature of their roles and responsibilities. What, for them, stands out as being key moments from their stories?

Across the decades: highs and lows
Practitioners had many stories of high points. These nearly all relate to their learners and colleagues, sharing successes and achievements that learners have made, experiencing the excitement of working in a field that is so worthwhile and satisfying, typified by the following comment.

> I always ... enjoyed it and believed in what I was doing. I felt that it had a value and that I worked with people who felt likewise. ... And there are levels of trust and respect that I don't think I've had since. (AR, Leics)

However, there were lows often related to structural issues, primarily around funding changes or loss of autonomy, and these stories powerfully show the emotional commitment to the field and the accompanying anger, sadness and despair that results from such changes to the field.

> I remember the terrible feeling of sinking and sadness and despair at the break up of the ILEA. And I suppose there is still something very sad about that, and somehow or other it felt like a big wave had come over the land and all you could feel, everything that had given you, made my sense of direction, was floating away or suddenly disordered. I think that was a very difficult time. Yes that was a low point. (CJ, London)

Tensions, reflections and action

We have argued in Chapter Three that policy action is heterogenous and can work internationally, nationally, regionally and locally. ALLN practitioners inevitably have to live with tensions resulting from their differing views of their context, and have to find ways to deal with the tensions through deliberative, reflexive spaces. We can see that practitioners do have agency, which is stronger or weaker at particular times and which we can see through their networking and activities to foster good practice and in the ways they responded to national initiatives such as accreditation. We can see that they have to manage tensions including whether they should strive for a coherent, professional system which is achieved through adherence to strict government set targets and standards, or for a diverse but quality service which draws together volunteers and learners to help define their goals. Even views of what goals are appropriate are a source of tension.

One tension arises from a reluctance to do the bidding of government, particularly in terms of meeting economic needs at the expense of learners' social and personal needs. Nevertheless, even those who were most stringent in their condemnation of current government policy in creating national qualifications for learners and practitioners, argued that it is important that learners do know what they have achieved, and should be given opportunities to gain qualifications. This also applies to practitioners, who should be given every means of support to ensure that they provide the best possible learning opportunities. Perhaps the field is so steeped in the culture of voluntarism that any hint of coercion is strongly resisted. Qualifications for practitioners such as the ITC, along with Wordpower and Numberpower for learners (see Chapter Nine), are earlier manifestations of the tension which continues under *Skills for Life*. Accountability mechanisms are subverted where they do not make sense in a practical context.

Where there was no practice or protocol, practitioners created their imagined worlds, for example in the way that they devised training, created materials and then shared these to foster a developing notion of good practice, all attractions for working in this field. Respondents worked in the new areas of accreditation, becoming assessors for the ITC or Open College Network, or managers who made decisions about which kinds of professional development would enhance their tutors' practices. They were not, therefore, the unwitting recipients of government policy, or even of ALBSU dictat. They could choose, and did choose, how much to follow and how much to subvert, but at times, they were powerless, particularly at regional level when funding forced closures, or later required certain kinds of activity such as accredited learning programmes to be delivered. Before they were forced to submit to the power of funding regimes, though, they organised student and staff activities such as sit-ins and petitions, and drew upon the media in their campaign to preserve and develop their provision for the learners (as we note in Chapter 11). Their position in the current *Skills for Life* strategy continues this active, deliberative involvement in local, regional and national policy implementation. However, the deliberative structures that would facilitate this have been diminished since the days of engagement through consultation, representation on committees and governing bodies. There might be consultation by the DfES, but the deliberative spaces allow little leeway for change of government aims. The compliance culture has become more pressing in the *Skills for Life* era.

In Part Three of our book, we begin to explore how practitioners have engaged with learners and policymakers as they developed, and continually changed their practices so that they could maintain their commitment to improving basic skills of adults.

6

The policy actors

'When you ask 'who made the policy?' *we* made the policy'. (JB, ESOL pioneer in Leics)

The ILEA though was an extraordinarily conservative place which was ... well resourced and ... everything went on that had always gone on but it was possible to create whole kinds of empires and subversive cells within it. And that was how adult literacy and ESOL came in ... so they were kind of struggling ... the organisers might be in an adult institute but most of the institute would be against the work. But they would be getting the backing from the centre of ILEA. This was part of the dynamic of it. (TJ, ILEA)

...the judgement they made that to defend literacy and numeracy work in the very utilitarian and skills ... focused work of the early '80s they needed to re-engineer the territory and to defend it or to present a face of it that went with the grain of public policy was probably right. And that if you see *Skills for Life* as a serious reinvestment in the territory then, whatever the price along the way, the Basic Skills Agency did preserve a national focus and voice to do that ... for people who are hoping for more radical critique to be there that's a real achievement that it's easy to ignore. (AT, NIACE)

Introduction

Who were the policy actors and how have they shaped ALLN by managing and promoting change? How far do institutional structures facilitate or block change? Here we look at the different levels of policy action that we outlined in Chapter Three, from international to street level. We examine the roles that were available to the different players in the field, the relations between them, how they moved in and out of prominence at different points. We ask what the policy actors were trying to achieve and their feelings about the roles they played as they worked with, or against, bigger policy forces and cultures.

We have already suggested that there is a complicated story to tell about how change has happened in the field of ALLN. Until the *Skills for Life* strategy, there was little that could properly be called national policy. This was in contrast to other countries, for example, Australia, which between 1992 and 1999 introduced a comprehensive Language and Literacy Policy that developed and integrated literacy, numeracy and ESOL. (See Lo Bianco and Freebody, 1997; Lo Bianco and Wickert, 2001 for a detailed set of articles about these developments; also Moore, 2002 for a critique of the ESOL side of this policy). We must look for change agents within local education authorities, in non-governmental organisations committed to developing the field, and to individuals who lit fires, spreading particular ideas and practices locally and sometimes into national and even international networks. As the *Skills for Life* strategy has unfolded, international influences that have always been in the background of ALLN have become ever more apparent.

Levels of policy action

We decided early on to talk not about policy *makers* but policy *actors* since strategic policy action can take place at many levels. We define policy action as any action that is intended to have an effect not just within, but also beyond the local teaching and learning setting.

Table 6.1 below shows the levels of policy action we have identified for ALLN, ranging from those most closely involved with day-to-day practice through to international agencies. In outlining the complex agency involved in turning policy into operational practice, we have drawn on Yeatman's (1998) useful divisions between different levels of policy, mapping them onto the ALLN context (see Chapter Three). We also use Yeatman's distinction between policy *actors*, who influence policy as a result of carrying out their routine role, and policy *activists* who are those with vision and commitments that they pursue across time and institutional boundaries, often in gift time.

The main players in ALLN 1970-2000

In Chapters Four and Five we noted how practitioners and learners engage with policy. Many of the people we interviewed held positions within local, regional and national agencies, either as employees or in a voluntary capacity, as members of networks and committees. Some were particularly active in these networks at times of funding cuts or reorganisation of services. These activities were not centrally co-ordinated but were nonetheless broadly con-

Figure 6.1 Levels of policy action and agents
(adapted from Yeatman, 1998:18)

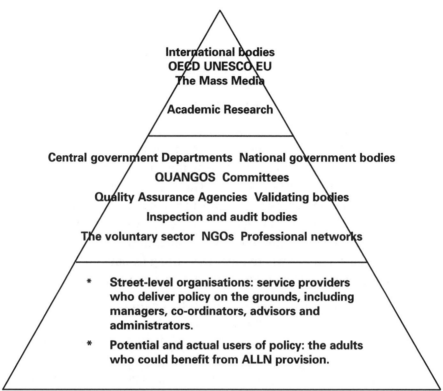

sistent with the developments that we described in Chapter One. We begin by summarising the main organisational structures and then discuss ways in which individuals moved among them.

A national agency for ALLN in England and Wales

The organisation that became the ALBSU and later the BSA was *the* lasting legacy of the original *Right to Read* Campaign and, as we saw in Chapter 1, has offered a space for policy action throughout the period. The original agency, ALRA, was directed by William Devereux from the Inner London Education Authority (ILEA). Despite the reservations of the BAS campaigners, it was given a safe home as a sub-agency of the National Institute of Adult Education (now the National Institute for Adult Continuing Education (NIACE). and this relationship continued until 1991 when ALBSU became a charitable organisation in its own right. The parent body played a supportive but somewhat remote and silent role in the development of ALLN, as the public presence for the field was energetically colonised by its quango offspring. The National Agency was constantly reviewed, its existence not guaranteed:

> Those first ten years of endless different lives for short life agencies with short life terms and conditions. There was ALRA for a year, then for another two years, then the Adult Literacy Unit (ALU) for two years, ALBSU for two years extended by a year and then for another two years, it was a crazy way of doing it. And nobody had any idea whether any of it would make any difference whatsoever. (AW, now director of the BSA)

Despite this uncertainty, during the 1980s, ALBSU's role as a central voice, presenting a public image of the field both to government and the general public, was crucial in providing coherence to the expanding field of ALLN and was uncontested on the national scene. Through its training events, newsletters and teaching materials ALBSU provided a national and international reference point for the field in England and Wales. We can see from our case study sites that ALBSU's importance was sometimes diminished by local factors, especially in areas where there was strong leadership from an LEA. This was particularly true in London with the strong presence of ILEA.

ALBSU took a major role in orchestrating subsequent media promotions of various aspects of adult basic skills, introduced accreditation at the end of the 1980s and obtained targeted funding for particular initiatives around Workplace and open learning (1990-92) and family literacy (1993-7). In 1995 its remit was significantly extended to include basic skills work in schools. Its name was changed to the Basic Skills Agency (BSA) and it lost its unique focus on adult education and training while increasing its presence in the area of intergenerational learning through families and schools.

Alan Wells has directed the agency since 1978 and it came to be identified with him. He was assisted by other senior members of the agency who had been part of the original activist groups, including the deputy director, Annabel Hemstedt (recruited from the Friends Centre in Brighton) and Gaye Lobley (formerly director of the ILEA Language and Literacy unit). Over the years, many practitioners joined the agency for shorter periods as regional development and project officers. The agency's royal patron (Princess Anne) and its management committee, whose chair was appointed by the government, provided both practical and symbolic weight. They offered the agency routes for communication and advocacy where these were not available within the democratic political process.

With the introduction of the 1992 Further and Higher Education Act, ALBSU seized the opportunity to have basic skills (already designated as an area of provision in its own right) included in Schedule 2, to make it eligible for funding within the array of vocational courses included in FE colleges. After the 1992 Act, ALBSU increasingly took on a quality control rather than a developmental function, introducing the Quality Mark in 1992 (see Chapter Five). With the advent of the new Adult Basic Skills Strategy Unit in the DfES after 2000, the BSA's power was much reduced.

The policy actors we interviewed present the BSA as being on the sidelines of government policy, acting energetically, sometimes critically, but at a distance from the centres of power. Practitioners, on the other hand saw it as being remote from their concerns, and more active in colluding with, formulating and carrying out government policy by selling out to the politicians of the day. Alan Wells always positioned the BSA, not as a practitioners' professional or networking organisation, but one that represented the interests of learners and of the field as a whole. However, since there was no forum for establishing what these interests were, the BSA had no mandate from the field and the director acted, ultimately, on what he himself judged these interests to be. It is evident from the ALBSU newsletters in the 1980s that the agency was constantly forced to pay attention to its relationship with central government since, as we have seen, its funding was only ever short-term. The agency had to establish itself within the constraints of existing frameworks and other organisations which we go on to examine below.

Other national players

The Departments of central government dealing with education, employment, immigration, health and criminal justice have been particularly important for ALLN. Tony Blair's commitment to 'joined up government' has meant that other departments have also been involved in the development of the *Skills for Life* strategy. In recent decades, there has been a proliferation of bodies, set up by governments and strongly identified with government policy in that they are funded by government and can only achieve change within the limits set by this policy. Setting up such bodies allows central government to influence policy without resorting to legislation.

A number of quangos have been important to the development and funding of ALLN. These include the BSA described above, but also the MSC and the TECs that later replaced it; funding, quality, inspection and development bodies like the Further Education Unit (FEU), the Further Education Development Agency (FEDA). Tracking the composition of the governing boards and committees associated with these bodies shows how the same people re-appear at different points. This indicates both the continuity in policy thinking and the limited range of people who were called on to take part in such groups. For example, Lady Plowden who had chaired the Plowden Report on Primary School Education was part of the group that organised the first *Right To Read* conference. Jenny Stevens, a BBC development officer for *On The Move*, was a member of the Bullock Committee that reported in 1976 and covered Adult Literacy in its review of English Language teaching (DES, 1975).

Setting up a committee can help central government work towards a change in policy and legislation. The committee and its deliberations are often widely publicised, they collect expert evidence and may engage in public consultation. We identified three committees of direct importance to ALLN, although there were many others that affected it indirectly.

In 1973 the Russell committee, set up by Margaret Thatcher, and chaired by Sir Lionel Russell, reviewed the state of adult education and made a number of recommendations which, whilst they did not directly change policy, affected the discourse and priorities of adult education toward what were then called 'disadvantaged adults', thereby making the field more receptive to the adult literacy campaign (see Fieldhouse, 1996).

The Advisory Council for Adult Continuing Education (ACACE) was set up in 1977 following the recommendation of the Russell committee, as an advisory body to review and promote educational policies for adults (see Griffin, 1987:196). It published a number of reports about adult continuing education, including one led by Richard Hoggart, well-known for his writing on the uses of literacy (Hoggart, 1957). The report reviewed the achievements of the adult literacy campaign and the national agency. Significantly, it argued that programmes for adult basic skills should be seen as a permanent part of the service for adults, not (as it had been seen until then) as a need that could be solved through a temporary campaign (ACACE, 1979).

The Moser Committee was set up in 1997 by Tessa Blackstone, Minister of Education in the first Blair administration. The committee was chaired by Sir Claus Moser, an economist and statistician, who made an influential critique of education and training in the early 1990s through the National Commission on Education. The BSA took a leading role in the Moser Committee's review of adult basic skills in 1998, acting as secretariat and providing much of the background research and other information. In this sense, the *Fresh Start* that Moser proposed was led, at least in part, by a key actor already in the field. Moser was shocked by his discovery of OECD claims, based on the International Adult Literacy Survey (IALS), that seven million adults were in need of basic skills help. His committee suggested a new national campaign was needed to address the issue and their report resulted in the *Skills for Life* strategy in 2001.

The Manpower Services Commission (MSC)

The MSC and it successors funded and shaped ALLN significantly throughout the period (see Ainley, 1990; Field, 1996). Its vocational focus directly challenged the traditional approach of the Department of Education and Science. LEAs were offered MSC funds to work with young people through the Youth Opportunities Scheme (YOPS) and subsequently the Youth Training Scheme (YTS). Parallel but much smaller programmes were funded for adults: the Training Opportunities Scheme (TOPS), followed by the Job Training Scheme (JTS), Employment Training (ET) and Employment Services (ES). Further education colleges, which had traditionally offered day release schemes for vocational training to young people and apprentices, found themselves delivering vocational and basic skills to target groups of unemployed people. A premium was given to trainees who needed additional support for their basic skills. The TOPs courses are strongly remembered by practitioners of the time as being the only full-time study opportunities that have ever been funded for ALLN. The Department of Education and Science contributed funds through the REPLAN programme (Groombridge, 1978).

Funding which fashioned provision had a lasting effect on the range of programmes offered long after the original funding streams ceased:

> ... because colleges and officers were pretty good at drawing on all those YOP funds and TOP funds and everything else that came ... some [provision] resulted from drawing on that kind of funding. So that also turned out to be quite a creative time actually and in many ways laid the foundation for what was to come in the '90s. (BP, Leics)

When the MSC was abolished, funds came through the national Training Agency and later were disbursed via local TECs.

Regional agencies

The networks and organisations with which street-level actors have interacted included LEAs, County Advisors, local TECS and, most recently, the local Learning Skills Councils (LLSCs). Often these regional players have formal links with national and even international organisations. Local structures were further reinforced through the Regional Advisory Councils (RACs), later abolished, but subsequently replaced by Regional Development Agencies (RDAs) in the late 1990s.

Responsibility and funding for provision for ALLN rested until 1992 with local LEAs. ALLN was inordinately dependent on and altered by the changing role and funding of LEAs during the Conservative era. Extra funding for LEAs came through ALBSU special development projects, and from accessing EU, DoE or Home Office funding. This money often came with conditions, for example targeting particular populations such as women, unemployed adults, migrant workers or particular neighbourhoods designated as in need of regeneration. These criteria changed unpredictably as short-term project funding came and went, and the fortunes of ALLN changed with them.

The institutional structures set up by LEAs affected local provision. Different authorities defined and linked their institutions in different ways. In Leicestershire, for example, an integrated Community Education service saw adults and children learning alongside one another in community schools. In London, the ILEA had separate Further and Adult Education provision, with vocational programmes concentrated in the FE colleges. Adult Education Institutes used school premises in the evenings and other community venues, such as public libraries. Norfolk developed a distinct adult education service, with centres dispersed throughout its rural areas and basic skills fully integrated within them. In Manchester the big FE colleges had always provided both vocational and general adult education.

The voluntary sector
A group of voluntary schemes, the British Association of Settlements (BAS), which initiated the *Right to Read* campaign, pioneered the use of one-to-one home tuition (see Fieldhouse,1996; and Kelly, 1992). The BAS had schemes in many of the major towns across the country, and these had traditionally engaged in educational activities and other good works with poor and disadvantaged groups. They were part of the radical social campaigning of the time. The WEA developed more broadly based *Second Chance to Learn* courses and many courses for women in response to the growing feminist movement (Edwards, 1986; Kennedy, 1997). Other trusts and charities like the National Association for the Care and Rehabilitation of Offenders (NACRO), and the Rathbone Society working with adults with learning disabilities, also became involved with ALLN. To the extent that these organisations depend on government funding, they respond to priorities in national or local policy.

In the early days, the national agency supported the voluntary organisations in the belief that they could offer something different from the LEAs and help pioneer new developments. Some authorities eg ILEA supported voluntary organisations but, when LEA funding was reduced, these organisations had a difficult time:

> For a voluntary organisation to not have statutory responsibilities or enormous reserves, lack of long term sustainable funding, it won't or can't continue. (AW, Basic Skills Agency)

People's wit and enthusiasm, though, played an important role in securing funding:

> And every year as part of getting our funding there would be an interview with a certain group of councillors ... and either all or one of the workers would go to this, argue our case and describe what we'd been doing and what we planned to do and we always got the money it has to be said. (SF, Manchester)

International bodies

Despite the absence of a clearly focused national policy, the interest of international agencies in literacy, language and numeracy has affected the UK. The EU, OECD and UNESCO have influenced the discourses used to understand the field, as well as shaping policy and practice through funding and research. These bodies are largely invisible and inaccessible to local players except through project funding or for those with links into national networks. As in other areas of social policy, however, the government tended to look to the US for policy borrowing (Finegold *et al*, 1993), and links with US were particularly strong, through research and through policy circles. The slogan *Right to Read* mirrored that of the US campaign during the 1960s. ALBSU organised a practitioner exchange with the US in the 1980s (See Auerbach, 1989) and a fact-finding visit on family literacy. Links were also made with countries such as Australia, Canada and Brazil.

EU funding sometimes made it possible for practitioners and students to visit other countries (see Murphy, 1990; Tomlinson, 1992). ESOL has always had an international dimension due to the student body, but many teachers also had overseas experience and training in EFL/TESOL. The British Association for Literacy in Development (BALID) and Education for Development were persistent presences throughout, organising courses for practitioners from a range of countries. They made sporadic links with UK literacy practitioners, drawing to them people who were interested in making links with literacy work internationally and analysing literacy as a global issue.

International agencies continue to be active and influential in the field. They promote globalising educational goals through international assessments and developing vocational, language-related and educational achievement frameworks to harmonise standards across the EU countries and beyond (see Lisbon European Council, 2000). Each of the major international bodies has worked in a different way.

UNESCO was a strong reference point for the discourse of the initial *Right to Read* campaign, adding credibility and functional definitions for adult literacy. Governmental links with UNESCO were disrupted during the 1980s and 1990s when the UK withdrew and initiatives such as International Literacy Year in 1990 were low-profile in the UK. The influence of UNESCO has always been as much symbolic and discursive as it is material, given its low budgets and lack of executive power. It nevertheless offers a strong reference point for governments around the world and is increasingly linked with OECD agendas for research and policy. It promoted lifelong learning through a major international conference in 1997 and ran world congresses on adult education, millennium goals and women's education (UNESCO, 1997).

European Union (EU) funding was frequently acknowledged by the practitioners we interviewed as a key influence on their work. Apart from the volume of support and the way the funding was targeted at specific groups, the project-based funding mechanisms, auditing and other paperwork requirements were extremely influential in shaping both the content and day to day experience of practitioners in literacy programmes. Regional development was crucially dependent on ESF funding which, in the early days, was less prescriptive than the competitive tendering of the late 1990s. It was appreciated by organisers and managers who were trying to maintain provision by drawing down these important sources of funding:

> [The funding] didn't have all the constraints that came later ... There was a lot of money around at that time. It was quite wonderful. You felt you could do anything. It really was the most exciting period of time in that work because you really could do quite innovative things. (MO, Manchester)

The OECD

OECD has been an increasingly important influence on ALLN (see OECD/ CERI, 1973; Benton and Noyelle, 1992), culminating in the series of nationally funded studies carried out in the 1990s that have produced the international league table, IALS. The OECD co-ordinated the IALS which produced the figure of seven million adults in need that has underpinned the current *Skills for Life* policy (OECD, 1997; Moser, 1999). Adult literacy fits into a bigger policy discourse vigorously promoted by the OECD that fits literacy and numeracy into wider educational, language and economic policy. This is expressed through think-tank discussion papers, survey research and a wide range of statistical indicators and international league tables describing the performance of countries in key areas. With UNESCO, it strongly promoted the idea of lifelong learning in the 1990s, echoes of which could be seen in New Labour policy.

Legitimising policy: the role of research and the mass media

We see the mass media and research largely as agents of discursive power, offering high status warrants that legitimise certain policy claims and ways of doing things. They articulate, publish and make visible certain kinds of narrative and evidence. Research can inform policy and change the terms of debate. In practice, however, it often functions to justify and rationalise policy decisions that have already been decided in principle.

Apart from a handful of pioneering academics, universities have had a minimal and distant relationship with the field, seeing it as part of non-advanced education and dubious about its legitimacy as a subject of research. Practitioners for their part mainly developed a pragmatic, working knowledge that did not pay much attention to research or theory and the national agency did not encourage links with the academic community. Practice-based networks, professional development and research activities were supported by Lancaster, Goldsmiths College, London and Leicester Universities, especially through the RaPAL network (created in 1985) and ALM (created in 1984).

Some practitioners documented and reflected on their practice through theses written as part of their MA or PhD level work (see for example, Jepson, 1990; Howard, 1994; Hartley, 1992; Hillier, 1994; 1998, Lobley, 1989; Moss, 1988). There were also small- scale research projects funded by local bodies (eg ALFA Clarke, 1989; Moss, 1988) and rare examples of voluntary organisations or students themselves documenting their own activities (Pecket Well College, 1989; Students of Blackfriars Settlement Literacy Scheme, undated). The Lee Community Education Centre, through its attachment to Goldsmiths College, had a self-consciously research and practice mission and is therefore one of the best-documented voluntary programmes (Mace, 1981; Norris, 1984).

Since the important role played by the BBC in the *Right to Read* campaign, the mass media have been used by practitioners and policy actors alike in a wide range of ways to raise public awareness and to construct images of learners, as well as to explore the possibilities of teaching and supporting learning at a distance (see Chapter Ten). They have brought in different ideologies of promoting basic skills that are not so entrenched in educational ways of thinking. Activists have always been skilful at hooking into the media in whatever ways they could, especially the local media, and recent government campaigns like the *National Year of Reading* and *Get On!* have explicitly encouraged this.

How people moved through the field

Policy activists, in Yeatman's terms, found their own ways to relate to the organisational structures noted above and move into the spaces they offered (Yeatman, 1998). We identify below the main strategies people used and some of the individual trajectories that people took through the field. The stories we have gathered relate to the description of who the practitioners are, outlined in Chapter Five. Here, we are interested in how their actions influenced the field.

The original *Right To Read* campaign made use of the parliamentary process to get recognition for an issue that was not on the government agenda, persuading an MP to put forward a private members bill. MPs were lobbied for a variety of purposes and were instrumental in publicising complaints about political bias in the field (see for example Mace,1979, in connection with the *Write First Time* collective and issues at the Friends Centre, Brighton).

Over the years, however, practitioners as a group were less active nationally in advocacy than their counterparts in, for example, Canada or Australia. In all the case study areas we looked at, there were local protests where practitioners employed direct action in the form of organised protests against funding, pay and conditions. Local managers and learners sometimes joined in these, but stable national networks did not emerge. Though many individual practitioners worked for national agencies over the years, on specific projects or as staff members, the agencies rarely invited consultation with the field and were generally seen as being inaccessible. As we noted above, ALBSU, for example, did not have any representative process at grass-roots level. Its management committee was appointed and some of its members had links in local networks. ALBSU Regional Development Officers visited local programmes and were a conduit of information in both directions. Independent organisations and networks voiced issues from a practitioner's point of view, and fed ideas and directives from the national to the local networks. ESOL was better served than literacy or numeracy, with NATECLA acting as a professional association, inputting regular responses to policy and actively shaping accreditation for both learners and practitioners, and the core curriculum for ESOL. The adult basic education special interest group in NATFHE collapsed in the early 1990s and in any case had difficulty in reaching the numerous part-time tutors and volunteers. The Research and Practice in Adult Literacy group (RaPAL) began to take on this role in the late 1990s because of the absence of any other group to do so. There was never a policy voice for numeracy practitioners, although Adults Learning Mathematics (ALM) provided an important networking space. Training networks such as The Workplace Basic Skills Network and the National Open College network offered valuable contacts beyond the local.

One aspect of activism involved working mundanely through committees and governing bodies. A committed head of college or area co-ordinator could make all the difference to keeping ALLN issues on the agenda. As one put it:

> you can support things strongly, or you can just let them happen ... you can influence by being seen to actively support that part of the work. That doesn't mean to say you have to do other parts down, but you can give out a message as a manager ... everybody enjoys a bit of support and feeling valued ... they were an incredibly dedicated lot of people, so it was very easy to want to help and support them. (DG, Manchester LEA College Principal)

Given the complexities and vagaries of funding, the pursuit of resources to support or enable specific developments to take place is a crucial kind of activism. Networking within local and LEA organisations to generate specific developments in practice and policy was part of this process and practitioners, local and regional actors became extremely skilled and successful in working in these ways:

> There was a small tier of LEA officials who were responsible for policy and knew nothing about adult basic education that they were making policy on ... that was what used to rile us so much. And that was why we ... side-stepped them and got to the councillors because we had enough political knowlege to know that the officers were controlled by councillors..
>
> Int: So you used the councillors as advocates really?
>
> Yes ... definitely, that's how we got the policy changes. We would not have got them from those officials. (JE, Manchester)

Finally, there were those who worked hard to articulate new understandings and ways of talking about the field. They argued for developments that they believed made sense but were not part of current public discourse. Sometimes this involved crafting local policy strategies, sometimes working through the media or in tandem with researchers to provide hard evidence whether based on statistics or testimonials from adult learners.

Journeys through the field

From interviews and documentary evidence we examined the trajectories that people typically took through the field, looking back on the experiences of those who came to play key policy roles during the *Skills for Life* strategy. ALLN has been a site of activity around which people with varying aspirations converge. It has been a particular focus for those concerned with social justice who believe that language, literacy and numeracy play crucial roles in cultural and social exclusion, people who are interested in working with adults to develop flexible, non-school-like, open systems for lifelong learning.

Some people we interviewed remained practitioners for many years, moving from part-time to full-time work, project to project, sometimes taking on middle management responsibilities, making the same committed changes each time in a new programme. These people contributed to a wide range of specific developments including research and we see them as working across contexts in a horizontal way. Some became identified with particular local projects including some that became extremely influential organisations in their own right, such as the Language and Literacy Unit, started by ILEA.

Many practitioners became locally involved with training activities, and from this developed links in county, regional or national networks that enabled them to work on a larger canvas. There were opportunities to become involved with national accreditation or quality initiatives and this opened other doors, including media and research links. People also moved into ALBSU other national agencies in the post-school sector, including the funding, advisory and professional development bodies such as the FEFC, the TECs and later, the LSC, Learning and Skills Development Agency (LSDA) and FENTO. Some moved into inspectorate or advisory roles. Still others took on an educational management role with a broader remit than basic skills and in this way took their visions and experience of the field into a wider arena. Another route to professional and personal development was through involvement with higher education, doing an MA or PhD alongside practice. In some cases, people moved into full-time into university teaching and/or research.

Those who stayed in ALLN over the long term, frequently had intersecting interests with other domains of social action, such as anti-racism, access, disability rights, women's education, community development and publishing and international development. They pursued their careers by linking with these other related domains and advocating for ALLN from there. Others chose to move out of ALLN altogether into a parallel field of social action and often this entailed a move up the career ladder. In a parallel way, some people in other fields became interested in basic skills issues and developed a sustained involvement from a tangential field in research or broadcasting that has its own career structures and networks.

There are a few documented examples of people who moved from being students to volunteers and paid tutoring and management, and many more anecdotal stories. This suggests a degree of flexibility and movement between roles that would be harder to find today.

These trajectories and the institutional structures that frame them are strongly patterned by gender. Practitioners, as we have noted, are overwhelmingly female, whilst the advisory and inspectorate, senior management and policy roles in the education and training sectors are dominated by men, many of whom started out in administration, rather than teaching. This is consistent with what is known about the labour structure of education and training more widely and FE in particular (Ozga, 1993; Newman, 1994; Deem, 1981; Avis, 2001). Women have made inroads into non-traditional areas, including research and training, and used their expertise in new roles. The rapid developments set in train by the *Skills for Life* strategy have galvanised many experienced people from earlier eras into new and different positions of responsibility.

Emerging issues and debates

The relative power of the media, voluntary agencies, local and national government to affect ALLN, changed significantly over time. These changes have to be understood in the context of both the maturing of the field itself, and of government strategies to manage a shifting political, cultural and economic climate. In the 1970s, it was the pioneering energy of the media and voluntary agencies that carried the field along. As local and national government structures were set up, the media and the voluntary sector took direction from these. The voluntary sector became progressively more marginal, partly because changes in education and social policy left them financially vulnerable but also because their role, as catalysts for change, gave way to mainstreamed statutory provision. In the middle years, the field developed haphazardly as it was carried on the currents of vocational training, programmes for unemployed adults and European funding initiatives.

Funding has been a particularly strong lever of change, promoting some aspects of the field and holding back others. The informal role of practitioners and learners as change agents is more complicated to track but we have ample evidence of their involvement from our interviews at many different levels within organisational structures. Practitioner activism kept many programmes alive.

ALBSU (BSA) has been the official national voice for the field in England and Wales throughout. The changing official remit and discourse of ALLN can be tracked through ALBSU's publications and even its change of names during different periods. It significantly shaped the way the field was viewed by government, and relations between policy, practice and learners right up to the advent of *Skills for Life* after 2000. We see the broadening of the field to include numeracy and ESOL and the adaptation of the discourse to the 'basic skills' terminology for the workplace and for family learning. The discourse changed as the struggle between the Departments of Education and Employment impacted on how the field was defined, and later as the *Skills for Life* strategy gathered momentum. The national agency survived by steering a pragmatic course between the field and the often damaging and incompatible government agendas that impacted on it.

Forces from outside the immediate field of ALLN acted strongly upon it. In the case of the MSC and the EU, their control of scarce funding during the 1980s and early 1990s was important and inevitably skewed provision towards their policy priorities (especially vocational learning) and target groups (especially women and unemployed adults). Numerous short-lived initiatives have influenced what we have described as forces for change. Working in a marginalised field, practitioners and policy actors have had to look to other social projects and sources of funding.

The international agendas of the European Union, UNESCO and the OECD significantly influenced the discourse of national government, for example in promoting the idea of lifelong learning in the 1990s, funding many initiatives aimed at harmonising education and training, and reshaping approaches to accountability and the financing of public services more generally. The extent to which these influences were understood by practitioners is not clear. They certainly accessed European funding, spending many hours writing applications to comply with EU criteria. They used the results from the national and international surveys to lobby for funding locally. However, few people talked about the effects of international policy during our interviews with them.

Tensions emerged from the efforts of policy actors to make literacy, numeracy and ESOL fit in with other social policy agendas. Choices had to be made as to how to use and create useful institutional structures that could also ensure accountability. These choices determined the shape and scope of the field in both intended and accidental ways, as, for example, in the original decision to place the field under the auspices of NIACE and to name it as part of liberal adult education. The lack of national policy attention that characterised the field for many years led to dependency on local authorities that led firstly to uneven development across the country and later to its decimation in many areas during the conservative years, as LEA funding and powers within education were reduced by central government.

The record of creating deliberative space within ALLN by formal agencies is a poor one. The mass media campaigns did promote public debate, but there was little consultative process and networking at any stage and policy was more likely to disrupt than to consolidate the informal networks. Whatever its strengths in other respects, ALBSU was definitely not a networking organisation and in its later years increasingly took on a quality control role, having dropped its regional training programme. It did not try to open up deliberative spaces for either practitioners or learners or even the general public during the conservative era. At this time, consultative space was almost non-existent for most students and the presence of practitioners on decision-making bodies was sporadic and discretionary.

The key committees that later affected the shape of the field (ACACE and Moser) were government-appointed and led by people with limited direct knowledge of the field and who therefore relied heavily on advice from civil servants, research evidence and information about practice that was filtered by others. They had little direct contact with the practitioners and less with the learners on whose behalf they were making decisions. This is acknowledged by both Alan Wells and Claus Moser, for example, as well as being mentioned by practitioners.

We should bear this legacy in mind when we look at the field today, assessing whether *Skills for Life* has opened up new deliberative spaces by creating new structures, such as partnership working, regional agencies, professional development resources and networks.

PART THREE

7

Spaces and places

I've been into so many school buildings and I've thought who in their right mind would sentence anybody to spend five or six or seven hours a day in this environment and expect them, you know, not to damage their soul quite frankly, let alone turn them off learning for a future lifetime. (SE, Manchester)

It was a building where the dock engineers used to go, it really was the leaky roof, bucket in the corner, there was nothing else available in that area so people made do with every provision that was there. (CL, London)

The mobile had what must have been condemned really, an oil boiler in the corner and you switched it on and the oil drifted into the bottom of it, you launched a bit of ... paper and set light to it and it went [sound effect] and it heated the room. And we used to run classes in there. (AO, Leics)

Met in a church hall and it was typical of its time I think in that you came in and you had to move all the playgroup equipment over to the side of the room, there were sort of folding card tables and stacking chairs and lots of people helped you get things out and at the end of the evening we locked up the building, we were the only people in the building, and left the key through somebody's letter box. (SS, Manchester)

ALLN has always taken place in an extraordinary range of places: in people's homes, churches, temples and mosques, community centres, pubs and shops as well as in adult and community learning centres and further education colleges. The early serendipitous days of ALLN where practitioners and managers found increasingly creative ways to enable people to improve their basic skills continue. However, key structural factors have affected the places in which ALLN operates (see Chapter Six). These include funding, local, national and international politics, and other social forces such as unemployment in the 1980s. We outlined in Chapter One how these forces rose and fell in relation to one another during the different phases. We now examine in more detail how they shaped provision and the institutional context in which ALLN took place from the early 1970s to the present time. We use the word 'places' in relation to the physical and institutional location of provision, and 'spaces' in terms of potential forms of provision that eventually could become specific places once they had been imagined into being. We argue that these places and spaces have been created as a result of the organisational location of provision, and that the initial low status of the provision helped reinforce the type of accommodation that was found to meet the challenge of this emerging field. Such provision suffered from changes to funding, particularly during the cuts in the 1980s, but was helped by alternative funding streams, and eventually through legislation in the 1990s which created a particular space in which ALLN could thrive and grow.

In the beginning

In his survey of provision in England and Wales in 1972, Haviland had found it difficult to calculate the scale and location of provision (Haviland, 1973), but his research established that there was provision in AEIs and technical colleges, 'private' programmes, prisons, borstals and 'other' (not defined!). The army had Preliminary Education Centres. The voluntary organisations offered literacy in small pockets alongside more traditional adult education programmes as in the Friends Centre, Brighton. Literacy provision from 1970, as we indicated in Chapter One, occurred primarily in adult education centres. Further education colleges had day release programmes giving assistance with maths and English in an ad hoc way but not labelling it literacy or numeracy. ESOL provision developed in various places, including people's homes, with funding from LEAs and Section 11. The major *places*, then, were in the community, but evolving *spaces* were developing further afield, becoming literally more concrete as institutional buildings rather than homes were espied for their potential use for adult basic education tuition.

> It's almost like a tree blossoming, or a flower blossoming in a way, you start off with the seeds and gradually little bits were added on. You started off with home tuition, you then had community classes in churches ... then it was into community education buildings and you would get support from the various community educators... (JB, Leics)

Creating spaces through adapting places

Although the field was developing, there is agreement in our data about the suitability of any location for basic education, and this specification helped shape the physical location of provision over the next decades.

> You have to have face to face contact, there is very little else that works effectively. You need to have somewhere what we call a safe place to start but somewhere where people can come without any difficulty, close to home all those sort of things, advice and guidance, access to mainstream. (RF, Leics)

One of the ways in which spaces were created was through the adaptation of existing buildings. Some traditional institutional provision was not appropriate and had to be changed or rejected in favour of sometimes unusual places. ALBSU (1984) drew upon local education authority reports when they recognised that:

> It is easier to attract adults in inner city areas to buildings which are seen as part of the adult world – community centres, clinics, pubs, social clubs. (Adult Basic Education in the Inner City 1981-1983, Sheffield LEA)

Given the immense variety of location, buildings and communities, urban and rural, across the country, we have uncovered different solutions to the challenge of finding appropriate facilities. Perhaps early on, community-based provision in urban areas had advantages; people were less geographically mobile, the community itself was more settled, and families could help look after children whilst a parent came to a local centre. In North East London, a Parents' Centre originally set up in a bookshop specifically aimed at attracting parents and families. Rather than being put off by coming into the bookshop, people who wanted to improve their reading felt able to do so as they could 'talk to somebody about the symbols'.

Another respondent found ways to create spaces by moving into the places where potential learners lived their daily lives.

> So every now and then I'll go and do a crafty session with a women's group or something just so I get the chance to talk. You get to chat to people and find out what they're thinking and similarly with mother and toddler, I'll go and sit in there for an afternoon. (AR, Leics)

Some of the spaces for ALLN were created through imaginative alternative ways of using accommodation which happened to be available at the crucial time. One respondent identified an empty room in a building shared with a hairdressing salon, and the organiser managed to get college backing to refurbish it, thereby maintaining their occupation of an important space in the community

> But we've been here for a long time. And that's really important here be-
> cause of the way the estate and the money that it attracts, people come and
> go so often. Agencies set up and six weeks later, or six months later, or a
> year later when the funding runs out they are gone, so trust is hard to get.
> (SS, Leics)

The need to sustain a presence in the community, particularly for voluntary
organisations, is an important issue. Lack of long-term sustainable funding
caused many tragedies of lost provision. Alan Wells argued that 'it would have
been better in the first place to give some of these organisations a guaranteed
five years funding with a review after five years'.

Challenging places

Not all locations were appropriate for learners, or even tutors. Because the
field was developing from nothing, with no rights or dedicated spaces,
accommodation was often poor, signalling the low status of the work. The
places in which organisers worked were just as inappropriate as some of the
learning environments that their students were faced with. The joke about
the 'dusty cupboard down the corridor being the office for the basic education organisers' was made by many respondents. In our Norfolk case study:

> One of the extraordinary things was when we went into the building in the
> centre of the city and acquired a photocopier, the basic skills team were in
> and out of the door like rabbits. (BG, Norfolk).

This manager was able to acquire rooms from the youth service simply by 'a
criminal act' of occupying them, and gradually created a suitable office for
the basic education team who had, until then, worked from their homes.
Another organiser used the boot of her car as her office and even interviewed
people inside her car! One organiser managed to encourage women to come
to the local community centre for ESOL classes by arranging to transport
them by car, but often found herself waiting while they 'nipped into a local
shop' on the way, taking advantage of their comparative freedom on those
afternoons.

Rural areas: challenges and opportunities

Two of our case study regions comprised rural areas, cities and county towns.
The demands of creating provision in rural areas reflected the challenges for
any public service including availability of public transport; low density of
population and therefore low demand; issues of confidentiality; and tensions
about local accommodation.

Everyone knew everyone else's business and no one would admit to having difficulties with literacy. There were no anonymous places to go. (MH, Leics)

If you are living out in the Fens in the rural parts, I mean some buses they go one way on a Tuesday one week and might come back the Tuesday the next, ... or they may go in on a market day, into the market town. (SB, Norfolk)

Sometimes, people who learnt primarily in urban areas were fortunate enough to go to a rural area or university campus for a writing weekend. The sheer delight of being able to live together over a sustained period, in beautiful surroundings, was a privilege that few students experienced, but nonetheless it was possible to imagine running basic education in a different format, and definitely in a different place. However, urban areas afforded their own opportunities, where respondents made trips to galleries, theatres and community centres. The idea that classes had to run inside a traditional classroom was therefore challenged, and tutors ensured that their learners could take their basic skills activities outside, reinforcing the idea that literacy, numeracy and language really were social activities which permeate much of daily life.

Having begun to occupy places and search for spaces in the 1970s, ALLN continued to develop, expand and move into a growing number of areas, as we now describe in the middle years of our story.

Organisational influences on provision: structure and funding
The middle years
As ALLN developed in the 1980s, it became clear that provision, and in particular physical facilities, reflected the organisational nature of post-compulsory education, and ALLN grew to occupy accommodation accordingly. By the late 1970s ALLN primarily followed the adult education model (Jenny Rogers, 1989; Minton, 1991; Hillier, 2002).

When I first started teaching basic skills people used to come Tuesday and Thursday or Monday and Wednesday, we had 4 hours a week. We fitted into an adult education model which was the model for doing dress-making or learning beginners' French. (AW, London)

We can show how one of our case studies, Norfolk, developed its provision during this period.

If it hadn't have been for *On The Move* I don't think we would have got a service in Norfolk off the ground anyhow. And then when we were perhaps needing a little bit more of a poke along came the second programme and again it gave us a bit of a boost and we went on from there. (MC, Norfolk)

The region was inundated with offers of volunteers, but the service was given no additional funding, something that was 'typical of the Shire Counties'. The second stream of funding for ALRA enabled the recruitment of paid staff. Consolidation followed in the 1980s when the county was able to get additional staff through appointing a part-time co-ordinator in each area. Basic education was provided in each region of the county by using the local adult education centre. As noted before, a local authority's political complexion defined how much provision would be funded. Norfolk had a 'very strong blue political County Council' which did not value post-school education apart from FE provision. In the 1990s, Norfolk County benefited from a change in local government, where the ruling party was overtaken by Labour and the Liberal Democrats, who were willing to attach more importance to basic skills than their predecessors. The development in Norfolk of a structure for adult and basic education is due to the careful planning and strategy adopted by one of our respondents, who had been director of provision before he retired in the 1990s.

> I'm certainly very proud of the role which I handed over quite a large well-oiled machine which I, with lots of others, developed literally from nothing whatsoever, or virtually nothing whatsoever. (MC, Norfolk)

The places in which the county provided basic education, then, came about through funding, through LEA decisions about structure, and through the hard work of individuals, primarily managers and organisers within the adult education service of the county who seized opportunities and operated as street-level actors, who interacted with top down decisions at county and later national level.

Cuts

Almost as soon as the funding for ALLN had been established in LEAs, national politics strongly influenced and halted further development. When Margaret Thatcher came to power in 1979, spending cuts on public services were immediately announced. This was to have a profound affect on provision in LEAs.

> There was a period when adult education was cut after cut after cut from year after year after year, in fact nationally it kind of survived embryonically but in a very different climate. (AW, London)

Adult basic education in adult education centres was squeezed and, across our four case study sites, we have stories of activism to try and prevent the worst excesses of the funding cuts. For example, in the London borough of

Haringey, once the decision had been taken, basic skills was subject to swingeing cuts, and 'disappeared overnight', despite the protests of students and staff throughout the borough. The places – adult education centres – were closed down and reduced provision transferred to the further education college. In Leicestershire, literacy was funded and structured through the youth, adult and community service. The response of staff in the service during the cuts in the 1980s was to fight a 'huge campaign', but was unable to prevent losses. It was difficult for community-based staff to 'support a campaign against the people who paid our salaries'.

Growth through special projects

ALBSU contributed to LEA provision, helping to shape the field through funding 70 special development projects between 1980-1985 (ALBSU, 1984). Initiatives reflected the economic conditions of the time, so that analysis of special projects for unemployed people, for example, identified the importance of the location of opportunities.

Where courses for unemployed adults are based appears to be an important factor in their success. A central location near the Unemployment Benefit Office or Job Centre has many advantages although if the accommodation is in poor condition, has inadequate space or poor furnishings, the advantages of good location soon disappear. The connection with education, is, however, desirable not only because of the other opportunities for more general education that are likely to be available, but also because of the general ambience of an education centre (ALBSU, 1984)

Two of our case study regions, Norfolk and Leicestershire, have been particularly active in family learning, a result of a BSA initiative in the 1990s. This provision takes occurs in schools and community centres, expanding once again some of the spaces of activity back to their original roots in the 1970s!

However, it is inaccurate to portray ALLN's use of place and space solely in terms of adult education institutions, as we now show.

In the work place

An example of a space that has continually expanded and contracted with changing economic and policy priorities is the workplace. The history includes both trade union and employer-led as well as government sponsored programmes, and throws into sharp relief the changing discourses and tensions of these years around funding and industrial relations, especially debates about who should pay for the training of low-skilled workers.

The first government sponsored workplace programme was the Industrial Language Training Service (ILTS) (documented by Jupp and Hodlin, 1975; Roberts, Davies and Jupp, 1992). This was funded through the MSC and later the Training Services Division from 1973-1989. It pioneered language training for ESOL learners in workplaces, identifying training needs and offering courses for English language learners and awareness of cross-cultural communication for fluent English speakers, for trade unions and for managers and supervisors. The 25 ILT Units run by LEAs in Greater London, the West Midlands, the East Midlands, Greater Manchester, Lancashire and West Yorkshire operated in factories, hospitals and other large organisations which employed people needing to learn or improve their English. They operated successfully throughout the 1970s and early 1980s but subsequently successive governments, uninterested in the anti-racist and equal opportunities agendas they promoted, were unwilling to take serious policy initiatives for ESOL, and they withered away. The ILTS is rarely referred to in current discussions about workplace learning. It was, however, a key initiative in the history of the workplace and ESOL and is a good example of 'institutional forgetting'.

Workbase, created in 1985 by the National Union of Public Employees (NUPE), was the most influential of the trade union sponsored education programmes. It began by promoting basic skills among manual staff at the University of London and funded itself through employers (mainly in the public sector) commissioning programmes for their employees (see Bonnerjea, 1987). It developed ways of working collaboratively with the different interest groups in the workplace, using materials and techniques of needs analysis which later initiatives drew upon. Later initiatives include UNISON's Return to Learn and the Manchester-based TUBE (Trade Union Basic Education project). One respondent who worked for Workbase noted how well resourced it was by comparison with other provision but, as with all other initiatives, funding was precarious, especially as employers were not obliged to fund training for low-skilled workers.

During the early 1990s, ALBSU put considerable effort into this area. It lobbied the government, unsuccessfully, to get the funding for Workbase mainstreamed. It funded and evaluated a series of workplace pilots, but these were not subsequently extended into more permanent programmes (Sargant, 1993). ALBSU also sponsored research studies that argued hard for the economic benefits of workplace basic skills, both to employers and to individuals. The Workplace Basic Skills Network (now The Network) started at Lancaster University in the mid 1990s. Funded directly by the DfES and a range of other agencies, it focuses on training ALLN staff employed by colleges to promote basic skills in the workplace and awareness-raising among employers.

Under the *Skills For Life* strategy workplace provision has once again been targeted for development, providing funding for employer awareness, research and pump-priming projects. Trade union learning reps have been a popular part of the strategy (see www.tuc.org.uk ; www.lancs.ac.uk/wbsnet; www.nrdc.org.uk).

Open Learning Centres

Between 1998 and 1992 ALBSU obtained seven million pounds of DES funding to set up 83 Open Learning Centres (OLCs) around the country, taking advantage of the government's enthusiasm for new technologies and the fashion for open learning within education more generally. The OLCs were drop-in resource centres dedicated to basic skills learning, well-equipped with micro computers and in pleasant accommodation. Supported self-study was offered in a variety of spaces: in traditional adult education centres and further education colleges which had rooms refurbished, as well as in city centres and high street 'learning shops' (ALBSU, 1991). Intended to complement existing provision, OLCs expanded resources for ALLN at a time when many existing programmes were severely threatened.

Prisons

ALLN had been an integral part of prison education even before the 1970s. Originally, LEAs provided staff funded by the Home Office and commissioned by the prisons. This structure meant there were differences across the penal system. The education system covered everything from basic skills through to Open University degrees. The inmates, though, had to choose between working for small financial reward, or studying for none. There were numerous disruptions, for example so that searches could be carried out, and the education offered was often fragmentary.

> We had about 150 women and my first job in the morning to get my class was to open the door into the wing and shout, 'Class!' and whoever first came to fill perhaps 20 places was my class. The following day it could be a different 20. (MM, Manchester)

Prisons, borstals and the probation service all provided ALLN, and the voluntary organisation, NACRO, acted as a referral agency in establishing need and encouraging offenders to take advantage of learning opportunities, not just for basic skills. The proportion of prisoners with low basic skills has long been seen to be a challenge for the education service. Prison education was contracted out in 1993 and further education colleges were keen to take it on. In our Manchester case study, this was to become a focus of activity, once the funding for ALLN in penal establishments was open to tender.

> We had a very innovative vice-principal who took the prison initiative forward and bid for quite a lot of prisons. In the first instance, we had three prisons which we later developed to twelve prisons and at that point were able to set up a prison education network that started to introduce concepts such as quality and standardisation. (MM, Manchester)

The college's involvement became extensive, with 22 secure establishments, 20 prisons and two secure training centres for young people (age 11-16) across the country from the North to the Midlands. Today, prison education is aligned to the mainstream practices of colleges, inmates are screened and offered basic skills and, in some prisons, given an automatic place to work towards their level one qualification. The inspiration of one prison governor has helped foster the social skills that offenders need, by working with the education staff.

> A prison governor totally inspired me and allowed me to expand the horizons of education in prisons. He allowed me to hold a wonderful disco in the gym where we showed the women you can have a good time without drink, drugs or men! (MM, Manchester)

Moving to different places: the FHE Act
The later years
We have mentioned in Chapter One how much funding affected provision. After incorporation in 1993, much of the traditional LEA provision was taken into the FE colleges. In Norfolk, the strong adult education tradition continued to operate outside FE provision. In London, the model of LEA provision continued, but FE colleges began to become more explicitly involved in basic skills. This was also because ALBSU began recognising and encouraging the development of basic skills work in FE, which LEA based organisers were not necessarily happy with.

In Manchester, there were agreements that the adult education schemes would run basic skills, and the FE colleges would operate more vocational provision, negotiating this locally within their other forms of provision.

> There was a totally new structure across the city ... what soon became very evident was that everybody was doing basic skills, you know FE was doing it in support of their vocational courses, but also probably doing some other stand alone basic skills which they shouldn't have been doing according to

the agreement as understood by us but it's a minefield really. (SS, Manchester)

Provision also fundamentally altered in regions where previously outreach had been undertaken by LEA schemes.

And the tradition of having outreach wasn't the tradition in most colleges and economically it wasn't. And the tradition of having rooms given over specifically to basic skills probably wasn't a tradition. (AW, Basic Skills Agency)

Some LEAs even sold off their community venues. Yet the FHE Act has also afforded enormous opportunities as provision is now free and funded through statute, with support for infrastructure and staffing. For some organisations, this has been a most positive experience, despite the bureaucracy. Embedded basic skills in vocational training was substantially boosted, and continues under the *Skills for Life* strategy today.

Places and spaces today

Organisers and tutors opened up spaces and thereby created suitable places but, as we can see from annual reports, the ways in which these are recorded do not do justice to the level and creativity of such activity. In 1986, the places of provision were reported as merely being in the Counties, London and Metropolitan boroughs, voluntary organisations and in Wales (ALBSU, 1986 Annual Report). The *type* of provision, whether in further and adult education, or work-based training organisations, was not specified at all. By 1998, the FEFC acknowledged the breadth of provision which included mention of 'Victorian houses, farms, smallholdings and decommissioned schools' (FEFC, 1998:10). Current provision, with the additional use of electronic resources, has helped expand learning into an even wider array of places than thirty years ago.

So we've four sets of laptops which we can take out and run, either taster courses or short courses in hostels, day centres, rehab units. (DH, Manchester)

Yet, as advantages accrue, challenges are created. For example, the increasing need for compliance with fire regulations has meant that some buildings have had to be changed, and one organiser found that she could no longer stick posters on the wall and create the kind of environment that helped modify the 'dingy and crappy' premises. Alternatively, buildings have become streamlined with all manner of facilities including online learning centres, coffee shops and drop-in advice centres, and are far removed from the adult and further education centres of the past. The understanding that learners require learning environments which are welcoming, accessible and of good quality has ensured that many learners today enjoy surroundings that their predecessors could only dream of.

Tensions

Today, programmes are run in drop-in centres, shops, libraries, community centres, adult and community learning organisations, further education, work-based training, in the workplace and in voluntary organisations. People can study in groups, individually and on-line. The places and spaces have expanded, and the times in which people can learn have moved to what is claimed by the *Skills for Life* strategy to be a 24/7 model of provision, although our learner interviews would suggest that it can still be difficult for individuals to access the programmes. What is clear, from our analysis of the last three decades, is that the early notions that low basic skills could be eradicated and that there would therefore be little need to provide an infrastructure has proved to be naive at best. Provision is dependent on funding, on political will, and on associated social activities, along with underpinning and often tacit views about who should be given access to what kinds of learning opportunities.

The setting up of an infrastructure in the early days was not straightforward. Here, tensions relate to conflicting views of the structure of provision, how funding should be spent, and how the field should be shaped. The resulting landscape is varied, partly due to the way in which particular views of ALLN influenced local, regional and national provision. Early decisions were key in affecting the institutions that were created and continue to operate. Tensions also occurred in the setting up of what were to become key agencies and influences on the field. For example, with the ILTUs, FE was seen to be inherently too conservative for the innovative work that ILTUs were required to do, and there was concern that provision might be stultified if located within the FE sector. This concern relates to a much wider political issue about provision which is supported by funding streams which are more demanding in terms of accountability.

> The FEFC and then *Skills for Life* have actually institutionalised these areas of work. That does make it less interesting and exciting and I think in all those years we were kind of pioneers on the outside of the system. I deliberately advised the Department of Employment not to put ILT units right into the middle of FE colleges because of their innate conservatism, their bureaucracy and all that. (TJ, London)

In the regions, many LEAs structured basic skills separately from traditional adult education. This created tension between staff employed in adult education and those in basic education, who saw basic skills staff running classes with fewer students, supported by the income made from more cost-effective courses with much larger numbers of students in each class. They made more demands for training and received a greater share of resources. Worst off were staff supporting the basic skills of their learners without recognition for it, for example in vocational FE. Later, there was tension when FE did become explicitly involved with basic skills.

We have seen disputes between providers in mainstream education institutions and private workplace providers, who were funded through the MSC and its successors, as we noted in Chapter Five. There were disputes about whether people should be offered tuition in groups in education centres or continue to study in their homes.

When the OLCs were set up, these islands of wealth received a mixed reception from existing practitioners, who were also suspicious that use of new technologies would replace tutors, isolate learners and exclude those who were not confident enough to organise their own study (see Bergin and Hamilton, 1994). They did, however, attract a new constituency of learners, including increased participation from ethnic minority groups and they were creatively adapted in a variety of ways across the country (ALBSU, 1993 evaluation report).

But there was agreement, too, about the need for flexibility of provision, and a sense of entrepreneurship, when organisers and tutors devised numerous ways to encourage people to learn. As we noted in Chapters Four and Five, staff and students occupied spaces when they were fighting cuts, by trying to keep hold of community venues that were subject to closure. They were, though, also invited in to decision-making, through management committees, steering groups and consultations, all of which ensured that there was a deliberate attempt to influence the places and spaces in which ALLN occurred. As staff found themselves working in different institutional settings over time, they learnt to adjust and found there were advantages, too.

> Because now we are part of a large organisation and we can fight our corner I think much more strongly. We have got a stronger position rather than being a community provision. (CW, Leics)

The effect of basic skills outreach work, and its utilisation of any appropriate spaces, has had profound effects, not just in the field of ALLN

> In those days we were the only organisations doing outreach work. We would work on tops of upturned table tennis tables in the village halls, and that's always been the ethos of adult education workers. But basic skills staff have taken that to the limit really and it's interesting to see how that's now seen to be something that everyone should be doing whether they are teaching IT, whether it's languages, we should all be working in a way that's kind of very diversified and accessible to different kinds of student groups. (BR, Norfolk)

The changes in institutional context have altered not just the provision, but the nature of the service and the way in which people relate to each other

> Leicestershire to me has always had a strong tradition of community education, the seamless road, cradle to the grave stuff but I think we did have that strong identity. The camaraderie and the good will that were there, we could run classes and not get charged rent. Or you could feel you could ring up somebody, 'could we have a cupboard?' I think that has now been eroded and obviously people move on, you get a new breed of education worker who perhaps don't have the traditions prevalent in the late 80s and early 90s. So I think the landscape has changed. (CW, Leics)

Funding streams have created the opportunity for provision to occur in a variety of places, and practitioners creatively used spaces to develop provision for learners. The tensions that have been managed in this respect relate to how best to enable people to feel comfortable in surroundings that may remind them of their early failures at school, or how to make use of funds that might have strings attached which are counter to the perceived goals of ALLN. It is interesting to examine how far the earlier pattern of provision has influenced the current landscape where emphasis is on flexibility of delivery but in places which are highly monitored and audited. Funding today is relatively substantial but with very strong links to outcomes, targets and financial penalties if these are not achieved

If we return to our five lenses of deliberative policy analysis, we can see that, in our policy life cycle, the policy of the FHE Act had a profound effect on changing the landscape of ALLN. The voices and silences can be found in the ways in which people talk about how they adjusted to new buildings and different places, or how they simply 'got on with it' in continuing to find suitable premises, or maintaining outreach work. This links with disparate actors, all aware that the provision of ALLN can take place outside institutional contexts as well as within them, even though such institutions were themselves changing in response to local, regional and national forces. We have highlighted some of the tensions that arise from working in the field, particularly around whether provision should be physically located in one institution rather than another, and what kind of provision that should be. As we have shown above, the deliberative and reflexive nature of the actions that people have undertaken, has led to influences across the lifelong learning sector, such as acknowledging that people can learn at different times, in different places and in different ways. People who teach, organise and manage ALLN continue to find exciting places in which to deliver basic skills and we are aware that these physical places are even expanding into the ether, through the use of technology. In village halls, community buses or ultra-technical drop-in centres, ALLN is flourishing, occupying any space that comes its way.

8

Curriculum and method in a student-centred field

There's trends when I look back at it. There was all this individualised learning and then there was group learning and then there was open learning in basic skills, then there was family learning and now there's work-place learning. That seems to be the latest bit of the evolution I feel, new students, new ways of working. (RP, Manchester)

People entering the field in 1970 brought with them a range of methods and ideologies from other fields. Nevertheless, perhaps more than any other theme in our research, being student-centred underpins the rationale of ALLN practice (Hillier, 1998). Definitions vary of being student-centred and how this works in practice. This chapter traces the development of student-centred provision and its underpinning theoretical roots. We identify tensions arising from different viewpoints held by actors in the field, along with the influence of educational theories and how these continue to affect the current curriculum for learners. The current prescribed professional development of practitioners is strongly linked to a student-centred curriculum, as we discussed in Chapter Five. The tensions around definitions of student-centredness are found in the hugely important area of assessment, which we go on to examine in the following chapter. The current term for student-centred is learner-centred, and we have used these terms interchangeably, as have our interviewees, following the acknowledgement in post-compulsory education that people are learners, rather than the more formal idea of students.

Part One: Definitions, challenges and development
Definitions
Any new field needs to establish what it does by defining its boundaries, specifying what it stands for and what methodologies can be employed to bring about its stated aims. This does not necessarily happen in a logical or chronological way. In ALLN, a major challenge was to find a methodology that worked with people who had not succeeded as children. The following section examines how the field evolved with its strong learner-centred focus, before we go on to trace the theoretical origins of its rationale.

The most obvious aspect of ALLN is that the learners are all adults who are assumed to make autonomous choices about their learning. The principle of treating people as adult learners is something that underlines the whole of post-compulsory pedagogy, along with debates over how to characterise the differences between how adults and children learn (Hillier, 2002; Fawbert *et al*, 2003; Armitage *et al*, 1999).

Practitioner definitions of being student-centred
Being student-centred, or learner-centred can mean different things to different people. The practitioners we interviewed specified particular activities or approaches, when they talked about student ownership of the curriculum. In numeracy, practitioners quickly realised that a curriculum without context was a waste of time, so being student-centred meant creating examples that were rooted in people's daily experiences.

> I discovered that trying to teach fractions to a group of women in isolation was a waste of time, 'a quarter plus 3/6 is equal to and this is how you work it' meant nothing to them. As soon as you started to talk about a quarter of ham or half a pound of potatoes then they understand what I am talking about now. (CL, London)

When practitioners discuss learners, they acknowledge their wide experience of life by the time they choose to improve their basic skills, as we saw in Chapter Four. They often come forward for help as a result of a major life change such as death of a partner, having children, being offered promotion at work, all of which involve them in having to use their language, literacy or numeracy in different ways. We also know that learners are referred by a number of agencies involved in public services such as housing, employment and health and ALBSU recognised the role that such brokers play as noted by our interviewees. The consequence of being referred, though, could either be relief to a learner that someone at last had noticed and could help them, or of threat, particularly if the referring agency was in a position to affect their benefits. The withdrawal of benefits if people do not attend classes has been threatened at times throughout the past thirty years, and was particularly prominent during the days of high unemployment in the 1980s, including pilots conducted to see if withdrawing the benefits from people actually made them do something about their low skills (RaPAL, 2001)) So we can see that not all learners were necessarily committed to giving up time to attend classes and, for learners in prisons, issues of voluntarism are considerably more complex (see Chapter Seven).

A brief history of student-centred curriculum and method in ALLN

Origins in one-to-one

Nearly all literacy provision was initially through pairings of a learner with a tutor, usually a volunteer. The success of one-to-one and its use was influenced by the Cambridge House settlement scheme. By the late 1970s, over 500 pairings had occurred there, as one respondent reported.

The benefit of this approach is working solely to the individual needs of learners on their own terms and, given a history of previous failure, many adults were making good progress with individual attention from a volunteer tutor, having spent their childhood hiding in the back of classrooms, or even truanting to avoid the difficulty of coping in large classes (Herrington, 1994). Tutors who visited people at home got to know other family members and a deeper sense of who the student was.

Students found it hard to drop out if a volunteer taught them in their own home (Sanders, undated). The use of community centres helped to dissipate such pressure although, in one example, a learner actually hid behind the curtains in a community centre because he did not want to continue with his volunteer, but did not want to upset her. Dependency worked both ways, where volunteers became so attached to their student they would not work with anyone else, and students gave up if their volunteer left.

Groupwork

One-to-one tuition was succeeded by group work, partly as funding became available to pay for tutors and to provide appropriate accommodation. Tutors, often with volunteer support, would work with small groups of learners where a low student staff ratio was promoted. A typical session for a group tutor working in a student-centred way would begin with perhaps a spelling exercise, that could lead on to writing at different levels to meet the mixed abilities of people in the group. There might follow individual work,

111

and then further group work, particularly for learners arriving later in the session. This mixture of group activities and individual work enabled volunteers to help out with individual learners, whilst fostering group cohesion. Groupwork exemplified the majority of provision in ALLN in the 1980s.

Group work has its challenges, particularly for managing the roll on, roll off type of provision, where students attend irregularly, and join throughout a term. Practitioners noted the frustration of planning group activities with a changing attendance

> You think you've planned something really good that was for six people and two people came. (JN, Manchester)

In some cases, institutional provision did not necessarily fit a student-centred approach, particularly in FE, where people had to enrol in September and, if they missed this, they had to wait a further year to join a course. However, flexibility of provision was a central characteristic of the student-centred approach, particularly during the 1980s. People would not necessarily come forward to improve their basic skills but would do so if they were learning a skill which they perceived to be of more direct use, such as cookery, or vocational subjects. Indeed, one of the key tensions in the field has been how to express basic skills in the curriculum and through promotion, and whether to teach people by stealth. There were a number of ALBSU development funded projects which helped to create new curricula to work with what were then called 'linked' skills, replaced today with the term 'embedded'.

Open Learning Centres were intended to help students access what they wanted, when they wanted (see Chapter Seven). As with other developments, the use of technology and a different methodology had both its champions and its critics.

> But the idea that people can just come in and work their way through packs with tapes or whatever, it sort of just destroys that, any human contact and the advantages of being a group, you know. (JN, Manchester)

In the 1990s there was massive disruption institutionally to ALLN, particularly through the influence of funding (see Chapter One). The wider influences of technology and accreditation changed the nature of the curriculum and methodology in ALLN. However, regardless of where learners met, they generally were taught in smaller groups than in more mainstream provision, and were increasingly encouraged to learn through individual programmes agreed with their tutors. The influence of meeting learner needs which typified ALLN had now permeated the rationale for teaching across post-compulsory education, as evidenced by the development of the teaching and learning standards by FENTO in 1999. We can not directly attribute this to developments in ALLN, although there was an interchange of ideas by ALLN staff on generic teacher training programmes.

ESOL

ESOL practitioners have argued that their provision is distinctly different from literacy. Learner needs are diverse, and the idea that these can be met within small group teaching is contested. For ESOL tutors, the management of groups involved not only issues around different levels of ability and experience, but other cultural issues that needed to be addressed to be truly student-centred.

ESOL practitioners argued that they are politically aware, because of the nature of the issues arising for their students. This was often demonstrated by the negotiated lessons arising from particular incidents, although this was not necessarily true for all provision. For example, one group dealt with a racially motivated murder in their locality by organising demonstrations and giving evidence to an inquiry that followed whilst, at the same time, other groups were working on 'how to make English cups of tea', hardly a political approach to learning a language.

Being student-centred had become an almost unchallengeable approach by 2000, even though everyday practice in the classroom varied widely. Wherever learners participated in improving basic skills, they would be encouraged to do so through focusing on *their* needs, at times to suit them, in places that were convenient for them, and with practitioners who had access to an increasing range of materials and approaches which claimed to enhance the learner-centred rationale. This dogma was used to sell the idea of improving basic skills to employers, public service brokers and to the general public and is now enshrined in the field through the use of individual learning plans (ILPs), despite an increasingly standardised top-down service.

Part Two: Theoretical roots

How did the student-centred approach become such a mantra in ALLN? One answer is that the field, being nascent, was susceptible to influences from other linked professional practices, which were drawn upon but also partially rejected in helping to solve this comparatively new phenomenon. Below we examine the key influences on the field.

Primary schooling

Practitioners were recruited from a number of backgrounds, particularly primary, remedial and special education. The teaching methods, critiqued as well as utilised within the early days of the field, were derived from other areas of education. The Plowden Report (1967) was a strong influence on primary teaching, with its recommendations on child-centred learning and recognition of exclusion. It is easy to see how people trained in this approach could transfer the underpinning rationale to their work with adults.

Further influences can be detected on the teaching of English to primary children through the language experience, or whole language experience. This was an era before genre theory was proposed, before the New Literacy Studies were articulated, when support with academic writing and learning, Access and Second Chance to Learn courses were just beginning. Established wisdom about language learning was being challenged. Whole language and language experience approaches in schools were being promoted by educationalists and writers such as Britten (1975), Rosen (1973), Searle (1971, 1982), Kohl (1976), and Smith (1966). ESOL teachers were being introduced to communicative language theories and the idea of a range of repertoires for linguistic expression. There were demands for plain English and to admit a range of expressions of popular culture into the classroom.

Numeracy teaching was influenced by the Cockroft report (1982). Much later in the 1990s, the creation of the National Literacy and Numeracy strategies in school were particularly influential on the creation of the national curriculum for adults through the work of ABSSU. Although the official reports and subsequent creation of curriculum and strategies for compulsory schooling have affected the structure, scope and pedagogy of ALLN, the actual content of teaching and learning developed independently, as we can see through the creation of adult appropriate resources.

Special and remedial schooling

Special education in the 1970s was reviewed through the Warnock Report (1978), which argued for including children in mainstream education. The half-way house for children who did not warrant a special education, but were not thriving in large classes, was for them to receive remedial education, or additional support in small groups or individually. Teachers in special and remedial education had developed practices that dealt with literacy, numeracy and, later, language. The influence of psychometrics was strong in these two areas of compulsory education.

Dyslexia was an area of dispute, still unresolved today, which grew during the period of our investigation. For adults, diagnosis of being dyslexic helped account for their lack of progress as children. Once dyslexia became more recognised as a syndrome in compulsory education, it was clear that it needed to be addressed in the adult population. The LLU created its own area of expertise in developing appropriate teaching strategies to deal with this, and the professional development opportunities taken up by practitioners influenced their approach to the curriculum and to the methods they subsequently used with adults considered to suffer from dyslexia. (Herrington, 1994; Klein and Millar, 1993)

English language teaching

Whilst the teaching of school children was undergoing its own mini-revolution with the influence of child-centred approaches and, at the same time, challenges to the way in which schools reproduced social structures (Apple, 1982; Sharp and Green, 1976), the influx of Commonwealth families into the UK from the 1950s onwards required a new approach to teaching English. The communicative approach to English (see Carter, 1997) was influential in the UK, whereas the multi-literacies approach was more important in Australia (see Hamilton, in Fieldhouse, 1996). Disputes about how to deal with language variety began as a result and continues to rage today. One major project initiated by ALBSU and then sponsored through the LLU was the Afro-Caribbean Project, led by Roxy Harris, who had been deepening his knowledge about linguistics in relation to Creole.

> I just did an ordinary language text written for adult literacy tutors who were mainly white British middle-class people who didn't know anything about it. Except that they would say to me there's a problem here and I don't know how to handle it, I don't understand it. (RH, London)

The initiative worked with individual tutors and teachers who helped develop materials and resources, leading to the publication of *Language and Power* in 1991.

Purposes of adult education

The literature cites two main approaches to adult education, liberal and radical. Liberal education argues for education for its own sake (Knowles, 1978), and radical approaches (Lovett, 1988; Westwood and Thomas, 1991; Mayo, 1997) seek to address the imbalances in power by empowering individuals through the process of education. Vocational education, particularly found in FE and the workplace, provides a more pragmatic rationale for learning as adults (Hyland, 1994; Bloomer, 1996; Ainley, 1990; Chitty, 1989). ALLN is practised in different ways, depending on how it is perceived according to liberal, radical, and vocational aims and purposes. For example, the influence of Freire (1972) is very strong and practitioners, when they cited their own theoretical rationale, mentioned his name over any other. Yet if we delve amongst the practices that our interviewees articulate, we can see that being student-centred represents all three approaches. Learners helped to read to their grandchildren are not seeking empowerment to challenge inequalities in society, or employment skills, whereas other learners are being helped to do precisely these things. Although practitioners may subscribe to one approach more wholeheartedly than another, they are eclectic pragmatists.

The major debate, then, for practitioners is whether learners best achieve their goals through a technicist, functional curriculum, or whether they are better served with a whole person approach which seeks to account for the reasons why they have basic skills difficulties and the effect on their lives. This debate affects the curriculum, as the following section discusses.

The curriculum

Initially there was no prescribed curriculum and tutors chose what to do with their learners, with huge variations in programmes. Some schemes created coherent curricula where practitioners interpreted a core curriculum created by their organisers. Centres ran dedicated short courses, for example, a ten week spelling course. Other programmes led to Access courses, and combined basic skills with a range of disciplines. Combining literature with literacy reflected people's lives where:

> This kind of learning is always actively part of people's lives and certainly the bits about day-to-day experiences of justice, injustices, discrimination, the humiliations in terms of the way people are treated, the expectations of them and their families, being looked down on, were always part of the subject of learning but so was the desire to view beauty and laughter, and the irony and all those very, very sophisticated and complex relations people developed through life, the coping with their lives. (CJ, London)

A fundamental debate in teaching literacy and language has centred on how much standard English should be taught whilst respecting language variety. ESOL tutors argued that grammar was a fundamental aspect of their work. Learners wanted to know about grammar and how to speak 'properly', whereas tutors were doing their best to respect the learners' own dialects and spoken language, a reverse of the accepted situation where tutors try to correct their learners' language. Family learning provision deals with grammar and issues of voice and register, simply because the parents want to know what their children are being taught. It links to work on critical language awareness (Ivanic, 1998, Carter, 1997) and the need to recognise language variety and focuses on technique and structure, even by those who had previously eschewed this approach.

The primary method used in the early days of literacy work, especially for beginner readers, was the language experience approach. This drew upon the use of *Breakthrough to Literacy* in primary teaching, and an understanding that people need to use words in their everyday lives, rather than working on isolated and de-contextualised lists of spellings. People were asked to talk about an aspect of their life, for example, their family, and the tutor would write a sentence in the learner's own words which would then be worked on for reading, spelling and grammar purposes, depending on the person's level of literacy at the time. As spelling and grammar followed this approach, it was seen to be a 'meta' approach which subsumed the more technical aspects.

> It took us a while to really grip that it was the absolute way to do it, there was only one approach and that all the other methods had to fit into that. (PL, Nofolk)

Today, in schools, and in the national curriculum for adults, the use of phonics is being promoted once more. Perhaps more than any other approach to teaching reading and spelling, phonics is the most contested in teaching literacy. Throughout our thirty-year period, its use has been rejected, subversively used and reinstated, seen as an alternative to the language experience approach, rather than one of the many tools that contribute to it. In fact, phonics has always been taught.

> And I think the problem was the fashion or faddism of a lot of teaching at the end of the 70s and the beginning of the 80s did nobody any favours really. Yes of course there were great things that came out of it but overall its effect was limited. I think if the research is to be believed we didn't do very well at it. (JP, London)

Another debate occurs in numeracy teaching, particularly in the use of times tables and other aspects of rote learning that have been associated with primary school.

Materials and methods

Whatever method was used in basic skills teaching, appropriate materials were required. The layout of a room, the kind of tutor and volunteer engagement and the latest available technology breathe life into a worksheet or book. Producers of materials cannot control the use to which these are subsequently put. One respondent told us of his evaluation of some of the materials created for ALBSU, and devised a scheme to categorise the users of the materials. The number one user, a 'surface user', followed the instructions, a number two user was a little more flexible through producing analogues of the original materials, and the number three user would be creative. This was exemplified by one of the tutors in Leicester who asked 'what's the tool going to do' and evaluated whether it 'taught the learners or simply amused them for half an hour'.

Early on, there was little appropriate material for adults. Indeed, in a survey of provision for adult 'illiteracy' in England in 1972, Haviland identified that 70 per cent of the literacy provision used children's books, and 80 per cent used material for 'backward readers', listing popular teaching materials all written for children (Haviland, 1973). This practice obviously managed to continue into the later part of the 1970s, as our case study in Norfolk shows, when an organiser found:

> 'Clumsy Charlie', 'Sound Sense', 'The Royal Road Readers', these are reading schemes that don't even have much credibility with children let alone with adults. And then when I walked into what was my office, a beautiful medieval warehouse, there in vast piles were Ladybird books. (P L, Norfolk)

A fortunate consequence of this dearth of appropriate materials arose from the BBC campaign which produced a tutor handbook and a student workbook. This was innovative for the field of basic skills, even though the BBC was known for its accompanying text books as in its language programmes. Later materials arising from BBC campaigns included the *Write Now* series. This programme worked with the Letter Writing Bureau and its then PR company which had a remit to increase the use of writing letters for the benefit of the Post Office, an early example of the involvement of a business organisation with the field.

Publishers such as the National Extension College, NEC, became aware of the market for literacy and numeracy resources. ALBSU published materials which were generally well received in the field, as did the MSC through Careers and Occupational Information Centre (COIC). Not everyone felt that materials produced by ALBSU, or indeed established publishers, were appropriate for the learners. One organiser thought they were patronising, and questioned why

> ...such an important segment of the population who has really got barriers and difficulties has to be given second grade publications. (MH, Leics).

Yet old, tutor-produced resources continued to be in use within schemes for many years after their creation. One of the problems with reliance on publications, is currency. Where there are limited resources, it is often thought that home grown worksheets have better value as they are more easily replaced. Our evidence suggests that they tend to last longer than the books! Tutors have favourites they cannot bear to part with, even if such resources are frowned upon, for example, by an assessor about to investigate a scheme for the BSA quality mark.

> This poor woman was clinging onto this really tatty book and I can't remember what it was but she said 'but I love it and I always use it'. 'But you can't!' You've got to hide it, they've seen it', and she obviously thought it was terribly effective. (SJ, Manchester)

Materials and resources need not always be formally published, although an ESOL organiser noted that publishers were not generally interested in producing books of materials as they did not think there was a market for them. Producing materials locally eventually provided the impetus for publishing through ALBSU, NIACE and the more established voluntary groups in Leicestershire, Friends' Centre, Brighton and Gatehouse. Avanti, a specialist publishing firm, became so successful that any basic skills conference from the mid 1980s onwards was bound to have a stall selling their materials.

We are struck by how the same skills and resourcefulness that practitioners were forced to employ in materials production continued to be used with each new wave of technology. For example, some of the best software was and still is produced for children and so needed to be redesigned or adapted with examples and presentation suitable for adults. We have lots of examples of innovations and of home made, individualised and adapted materials. We are also struck that the same constraints are apparent, limiting and compromising the promise of computer-based teaching and learning. Too few computers, or old and clunky machines; lack of suitable space; lack of secure premises limiting use of computers; dispersed premises meaning that tutors now carry laptops around with them, rather than the plastic bags full of books as before, nomadic as always, 'trundling those damn machines about'.

Given the ambivalent public discourse about new technologies, many of the practitioners we interviewed come over as surprisingly positive in their attitudes to ICT. They are willing to experiment with new media, to innovate, to train themselves and grab new equipment, to see what computers could offer students (see book by Freda Hollins and other special development projects on use of micro computers). Perhaps this is partly to do with having always been starved of resources and life being made so difficult because of this:

> [the ALBSU development project] was the first funny money that ever came to basic skills. We'd always got through on a shoe string before. One of my first ever projects was to buy a photocopier cause there was always a problem about the photocopier – how much paper you use and how much access you had to it. And the most liberating thing for a group of part-time tutors would be to have their own photocopier with nobody asking questions about how many copies you were doing. And so I think they [ALBSU] probably wanted a very grand project and I wanted a very grand photocopier! [*laugh*]. (RP, Manchester)

Today, the word 'curriculum' invariably has prescriptive connotations, meeting awarding body standards, or national requirements. The national curriculum in *Skills for Life* has been praised for providing a framework, or criticised for being too narrow, linked to school standards of achievement. From our analysis of the past three decades we can see that, over the first ten years, there was little accreditation and little explicit coherence or curriculum. It would be inaccurate to argue that accreditation created a curriculum, but it did help define it.

> Good teaching is good teaching and whether, if you are teaching something well you almost unwittingly will be teaching to the core curriculum. Almost unwittingly you will be working towards accreditation. (AW, Norfolk)

As we discuss in the next chapter, there was suspicion about the introduction of accreditation, and whether it would fit with meeting the students' needs and aspirations.

> I remember feeling strongly against any kind of accreditation. I said it would lead to a situation where people are examined and therefore we shouldn't have any of it. You know as if we should keep adult education pure and free of this contamination. (JD, London).

Student writing

Students were encouraged to write about themselves, to publish their work and, in some cases, to use their writing as a platform to challenge cuts in funding and provision, and wider policy issues of the day that affected them, such as unemployment (see Chapter Four). The student writing and community publishing movement was a visible strand in early work in ALLN and remains influential, if submerged, in current practice. One of the frequent stories told by our interviewees is about students drawing attention to themselves through their writing, and the concerns they expressed in it. There is a mythical, iconic status to the movement and its rise and fall has been re-corded well by Jane Mace (see for example, O'Rourke and Mace, 1992). An archive of *Write First Time* (a newspaper produced by a collective of tutors and students around the country) exists in the Ruskin College library and our own Changing Faces archive has many examples of the products of student writing and community publishing activities.

The student writing movement folded into one set of activities an alternative view of the origins of literacy difficulties, politically rooted in concerns about social justice, unequal access to education and culture; a solution to the dearth of adult-focused reading materials and an alternative pedagogical process through the scribing/language experience/editorial approach. The significance and radicalism of this movement stems from the dominant literacy paradigms of the day: approaches adapted from remedial reading programmes with children; a prevalent belief in the low ability of ALLN students; a belief that writing could not be tackled by poor readers, and that tuition therefore should be focused on the mechanics of handwriting and spelling rather than creative writing activities.

The curriculum content and activities of the student writing movement affected social relations in the learning situation. It changed how the teachers' role was perceived, now acting as mediator and scribe rather than expert (see Mace, 2002). It opened up new possibilities for the students' role in management and decision-making surrounding the teaching, learning and editing process.

This new way of approaching literacy involved demystifying the processes of administration and decision-making. It led to efforts to produce accessible minutes, newsletters and annual reports (see e.g. the NFVLS *wallpapers* and Centreprise and Pecket Well annual reports). It led to the invention of new organisational forms such as the writing weekend and the *Write First Time* newspaper collective, and forms of published output such as collections of short pieces of writing, a mixture of prose and poetry and graphics, drama and opinion and news items (see the CF archive for different formats across the time period in different anthologies). The emphasis on the production of writing, rather than just reading, audience issues, paying attention to line breaks and other aspects of layout, and plain English to increase readability, were revolutionary to the literacy field, mirroring wider political and cultural experiments of the time.

The student writing movement affected methods of advocacy for ALLN, in-creased the visibility of student voices and challenged assumptions about who could create literature. It was potentially powerful, therefore, as a shaping force in the field. Perhaps for this reason it was not allowed to flourish unchallenged and the fact that it ran into political difficulties reveals a lot about the dominant assumptions and the climate of the time. A number of criticisms were made of student writing: that it 'failed to combine itself with the teaching of the underpinning skills' that tutors were engaging in political 'brain washing' through encouraging the students to write critically about government policies, that the repeated autobiographical stories were boring, had little literary merit and were not read or used by other people. During the 1980s these collections were regularly reviewed in the ALBSU newsletters, sometimes by groups of students themselves, who gave mixed reactions to them: 'Brilliant' and 'Throw it in the bin' (see O'Rourke, 1992:12,13). Even those who strongly supported it suggested that it did not reach its full potential, as noted in Chapter Four. These difficulties, combined with the lack of mainstream resources for developing student writing activities since the mid 1980s, prevented the movement from realising the full variety of its expression in practice, especially in cross-curricular work, family and workplace programmes.

Part Three: Tensions and debates

If we examine the policies that have influenced the student-centred field, we can see that, in general, it is the activity of the practitioners that has primarily influenced the curriculum, and it is only in the *Skills for Life* agenda that the influence of a national policy is steering the curriculum towards a more centralised, compliant approach. Attempts to stabilise the problem of creating an appropriate way to teach adult basic skills is linked closely to our stage five, where the curriculum has been particularly influenced by deliberative, reflexive action as practitioners recognised that previous approaches to fostering learning for children were inappropriate for adults, and they created new resources and methods (as had the staff in the Preliminary Education Centres in the army before them). The tensions, however, that have arisen in the field continue to influence how people define and practice a student-centred curriculum. It is clear, though, that such practices extend beyond the field of ALLN to the post-compulsory sector generally (Armitage *et al*, 1999; Fawbert, 2003; Hillier, 2005).

Once the FEFC was created, learners were expected to complete a learning contract, stating what their learning aims were and how they were going to achieve them. The focus on meeting the needs of the learner, then, moved from an informal dialogue between tutor and student to a bureaucratically-

led system, with funding attached to recruitment, achievement and reten-
tion, culminating in the use of Individual Learning Plans (ILPs). This is a clear
example of how institutional contexts began to shape the student-centred
curriculum, which by this time was now using the term learner-centred.
Some practitioners, particularly those with organisational and management
responsibilities, attempted to keep this focus whilst managing the demands
placed on them by senior management, national policy and strategy, and
limited resources.

> We spent a lot of time working out how you might evidence progress in a
> more student or learner-centred, learner-friendly way than putting people
> through Wordpower and Numberpower. And all those difficult issues about
> special needs and all those funding issues about learning support and oh
> dear, dear, dear. MC, Leics).

A student-centred field, as we argued at the beginning of this chapter, is not
simple or homogenous, and its ethos does not reflect the underlying tensions
that have served to maintain the dynamic growth and dialogues found within
the field today. Early on, disagreements over whether people should be
taught on a one-to-one basis or in groups, served to lay the foundations of
different provision replicated across the country, certainly evidenced in our
four case study sites.

The current shape of ALLN owes much to the deeply-held belief that student-
centredness is an ideologically appropriate approach to adopt. This ideology
at times conflicts with the major influences on the field such as accreditation,
widening participation, ensuring adults are able to function in society and
particularly in the workplace, and globalised factors including accountability
and surveillance. When, for example, accreditation was introduced, the
resulting demands on practitioners highlighted the existing tension about
how to meet students' needs and provide an appropriate curriculum and
outcomes. For every positive response to the accreditation initiative, we have
found a counter-argument, and both would be contextualised against the
underpinning subscription to a student-centred framework.

Even student writing, which might seem comparatively non-controversial,
proved to be the reverse. It has been criticised for not providing the best way
to help people improve their basic skills and in terms of political control exer-
cised over students. Those who have worked with it in the past now re-frame
their views in the light of the developments in teaching basic skills, and an
understanding that it is only through additional teaching and learning
activities that the writing can help facilitate the knowledge, skills and understanding that people need to develop their level of literacy, numeracy or
language.

The new national curriculum for learners, and also the curriculum for professional development of practitioners, continues to challenge the diverse views within the field. The technicist approaches to teaching ALLN are included in the standards for teachers and we can see that these will continue to stimulate the long-debated questions of how and when we should be using phonics, times tables and grammar and punctuation. The acknowledgement of language variety is also far from established in the mainstream.

These debates will continue, but there is a need for careful research into which methods work effectively and under what circumstances. The work of the NRDC is a helpful way forward, and a social practice approach to ALLN goes beyond the purely technicist methodologies. Conversely, the taken for granted assumption that being student-centred is the only appropriate approach, belies the wide-ranging meanings this term holds for practitioners.

9

Mapping and tracking: assessment and accreditation

I was very proud that we took some quite hard decisions about using Word-power and Numberpower and doing work-based basic skills because I felt that we needed to move away from a model that clearly wasn't answering a lot of people's needs in terms of progression. (SC, Norfolk)

... then there was the whole business of trying to persuade students to pay money for certificates which really were valueless ... a vast number of those students couldn't really afford it anyway. (ST, Leics)

We tend to channel them down certain paths now and ... there's less emphasis on ... just learning for learning's sake and writing for writing's sake ... and it's more about skills ... It's more sort of skills for work, skills for ... life and things like that. (PW, Manchester)

If people want to improve their basic literacy, language and numeracy, how do they know they are making progress? How do the managers of provision know that the teaching and facilitation of learning is effective? If adults have experienced failure in their early lives, then are there better ways to help them make progress and find out their achievements than those they were exposed to in school? These questions inevitably lead to the hotly contested topic of assessment and accreditation.

The distinctions between assessment, testing and accreditation have become conflated in the current *Skills for Life* context. Assessment is a process of identifying what has been learnt, either recently or over a length of time, whereas accreditation is the award of credit, leading to qualifications, of learning which can be shown through the successful achievement of learning outcomes (Lavender *et al*, 2004). Assessment is not the same as testing which, as we show, has particular connotations for learners who have failed in the past.

Assessment is one tool which helps to establish the success of a learning programme. To ensure that the information is gathered, records need to be kept, for example of how many learners start or complete a programme, how long they spend in the programme and whether they achieve a qualification. So assessment and record keeping are part of the much wider area of assuring and enhancing quality, which in turn is located in the drive for accountability. For further reading on assessment see Armitage *et al*, 1999; Curzon, 2004; Fawbert, 2003; Hillier, 2002, 2005.

The early days of assessment

ALNE, whether in voluntary organisations, settlements or local authority provision, did not contain any formal assessment of learning as such, although it was conducted informally through discussion and feedback with learners. The non-formal nature of assessment was partly due to the fact that very few adult education courses involved formal assessment, unless they specifically led to qualifications, such as the GCE O Levels of the time or vocational qualifications such as Royal Society of Arts (RSA) Typing. People either came to classes because they had a leisure interest in the subject or because they wanted to use it for specific purposes such as learning a language to use on holiday. It was accepted that classes comprised a range of levels and abilities, and the onus was on the teacher or tutor to find suitable ways to engage learners across this range. Therefore, adults who wanted to improve their literacy, language or numeracy were originally all treated in much the same way, although there was great sensitivity around the fact that they might feel shame or embarrassment about needing to attend classes, and an awareness that they might have found any assessment difficult, due to their experiences of failure in the past.

> A school experience, which was re-told time and again in those stories by learners of humiliation and reading and writing strategies that had failed them. (ME, London)

It was almost anathema for practitioners to assess people, either in the beginning through diagnostic tests, or at the end of a course. Indeed, the idea of *testing* learners and putting them back into categories they had been hoping to move away from, such as 'remedial' or 'special', was eschewed in favour of giving people a fresh start with no preconceptions about their ability. One of the tensions throughout the history of basic skills provision has arisen from respecting people's nervousness and helping them to overcome it. As one of the NCDS informants put it:

> I am shy of courses that have an exam at the end of them, because I get terribly nervous and the mind goes blank. (NCDS P33)

To test or not to test

The use of tests is a controversial subject for any part of the education and training system. Although assessment can be done in a number of ways, testing has been rejected, avoided but sometimes wholeheartedly adopted by practitioners in ALNE. By the time people are adults, they may have been exposed to a number of tests, particularly these days through SATS, and GCSEs in school, or possibly the 11 plus, diagnostic and psychometric testing as well as the more mundane experience of taking a driving test. For many practitioners, testing is not their favoured method and their view is informed by their understanding of lifelong learning, people's experiences of failure and, latterly, the inadequacy of tests to provide an accurate description of what people can actually do.

> People used to keep asking me how do you test the students, how do you assess ... and I said we don't do that, that's the thing that would send them scurrying for a start, apart from which literacy is a lifelong thing we are all still becoming more literate all the time, our literacy is being developed in different ways ... The minute you start testing all that sort of thing, you then record figures and you start categorising. (CM, London)

> Diagnostic testing and assessment criteria was not appropriate, probably not even listened to, it was much more 'How did you get to this position?' 'Why do you have reading and writing needs?' 'How can we help you within your work?' (ME, London)

The story is more complex than this. In workplace provision, there was an explicit attempt to identify what the employees could do to match their needs to development that would enable them to work more effectively. One respondent, an ILTU director who worked with Ford, explained how the company introduced verbal and numerical reasoning assessments for its staff wishing to progress in the company, which a disproportionate number of black and Asian workers failed. Independent assessments of the tests were conducted and attempts to reduce the cultural bias were made, along with work-based provision for people during company time to help them prepare for a re-test with a ninety-percent success rate.

> So what Ford ran was a six week programme, people would attend in com-
> pany time for five mornings a week or five afternoons a week and at the end
> re-sat the assessments and I think probably fifty or so people went through
> those over time, and I think there was a ninety-nine success rate. (PL,
> London)

Cultural bias is one major criticism found within any testing regime and is particularly pertinent in situations where people can be discriminated against in employment or education applications. In another example, learners' motivation to improve their basic skills had resulted from failing a timed test for MSC-funded vocational training and, of course, tutors worked with them to ensure that they could undertake the test. Note here, though, that in both cases, practitioners worked with employees or trainees to pass tests, rather than rejecting the use of tests outright.

Prisons have used testing throughout their involvement in basic education, but the current system is more structured than previously, with diagnostic testing providing better initial screening tools.

> At the time we were frightened to death of the new screening coming in, we
> couldn't do it. It's now become routine. (MM, Manchester)

As the prison population is particularly mobile, some inmates are tested on numerous occasions as they are transferred from one prison to another, or change from being on remand to being in custody, a reverse of the original situation where no one was tested at all.

For the schemes which did reject testing, various practices ensured that learners were placed in groups according to the level of their basic skills. For example, initial interviews were used to place students and these were usually informal, but not totally random. Some prospective students might be asked to specify what they had difficulty with, others may even have been asked to try to write a sentence, or indicate if they knew how to work out simple mathematical problems like fractions. Checklists were devised where people were asked to self-assess by stating if they had difficulty in under-taking any of the items listed.

> We did assess people, we had an assessment process and we had a record-
> ing system for it and we had a way of offering people then the next steps. It
> wasn't required by inspectors or officers or even our own settlement, we did
> it in some cases through the voluntary schemes network, through the
> National Federation of Voluntary [Literacy] Schemes. (JP, London)

Ongoing assessment

The idea that there was no ongoing assessment at all in the early days is inaccurate. In some areas, good practice was being developed and then, typically, taken up by ALBSU and proselytised in the field, usually with a publication such as *How's it going?* by Martin Good. Here, tutors were encouraged to identify people's current level of skill and knowledge in a structured way, as well as identifying what could then be developed.

> *How's it going?* did two things; it needed to be informative and it helped codify practice. Being formative so you could get a sense of how good you were in the overall sense and also an action plan for things that you might want to start learning was the best feature of the scheme that we were running. (MG, CTAD)

In 1989, Deryn Holland was contracted by ALBSU to work on a more coherent identification of learner goals and she created the Progress Profiles (ALBSU, 1989). This would anticipate the demand for establishing how effective learning programmes were. The Progress Profiles did not become fully incorporated into ALNE, partly because of the development of formal qualifications within the following year (see below), and also because the profiles were very bureaucratic, using 'five pages of paper' (AW, London) which proved to be unsustainable.

A plethora of qualifications

A range of qualifications existed in the early 1980s which were used by ALNE tutors for their learners. Two major awarding bodies, RSA and City and Guilds, had qualifications in language, communication skills and numeracy. The RSA had its Certificate of Continuing Education (CCE) which was in many ways a pre-curser to an outcomes-based framework. Initially, ESOL learners could gain credit as there were examinations in English Language proficiency for EFL learners. For numeracy, there were a number of established routes to qualifications through City and Guilds or the RSA. Because maths is seen by many to be a more structured discipline, it was assumed that learners could fit more easily into levels and therefore be aware of the progress they could make, for example, through the City and Guilds awards which were set at levels one and two. The ILEA introduced a mathematics scheme which involved learners in diagnosing what they needed to learn in order to gain the important O level in maths required for primary teaching. This was in its last stages of preparation for publication when ILEA was disbanded. The art work for the scheme is held in the Changing Faces archive. The idea that numeracy and maths is somewhat easier to assess is not universally accepted (Coben, 2003).

The range of qualifications available for learners in post-compulsory education and training was precisely the problem which led to the creation of
NCVQ, in that it was hard for anyone outside the field to understand what
qualifications existed, what they claimed to represent in terms of level and
achievement, and how they could be used towards further study or employment. Qualification for ALNE was simply subsumed within this problem, and
the ensuing development of Wordpower and Numberpower was a decision
typical of its time.

> We had a slightly similar experience when key skills were being created, in
> saying to NCVQ as it was at the time, 'why are we recreating yet another
> version, we have got communication skills, we have got Wordpower and
> Numberpower why do we need this new thing?' So yes there was a tension.
> (TF, Awarding Body)

Ironically, the new qualifications *added* to the qualifications jungle (see
Hillier, 2002), and the status and benefits of such awards continue to be mis-
understood by politicians, the general public and employers today. In 1991,
almost 10,000 learners gained a City and Guilds qualification in Communication Skills, and only 17 in Wordpower but, by the year 2000, there were 2,000
certificates in Communication Skills, 18,000 Numeracy certificates but also
24,000 Wordpower and Numberpower awards, all of these awards aimed at
accrediting the same level of basic skills.

BSAI, Wordpower and Numberpower

In 1989, ALBSU, together with the BBC, began the Basic Skills Accreditation
Initiative, and included consultations before defining the format of the qualification that was to become Wordpower and Numberpower. The BSAI proved
to be one of the most contested aspects of ALNE in the 1990s. Learners might
have liked the idea of working towards a qualification, but tutors were not
convinced of its value, and some even argued that their learners hated it too.
RaPAL reported a number of surveys on learners' views of accreditation, providing welcome data to support the field in its management of the tensions
surrounding accreditation (see O'Rourke *et al*, 1992; Whitty, 1993)

The introduction of the accreditation initiative was not government led and
was introduced after consultation even though the Director of ALBSU was
aware that a large number of people were against it.

> Well the peculiar thing about it which is that sometimes of course opposition
> gives you more courage than almost anything else. You sometimes have a
> belief in the values. Interestingly in terms of Wordpower and Numberpower
> it was immensely popular with the learners, they liked it. (AW, London)

One view of how the two qualifications came into being describes, additionally, the national context at the time. NVQs were being developed as a result of the 1981 White Paper on vocational qualifications and the setting up of the NCVQ in 1986 (see Hillier, 2002, Hyland *et al*, 2003). Thus the driving force was through government, but in the form of the MSC or Training Agency, as it had become

> I would say that during that period, because I was working largely for the Manpower Services Commission and its successors that the real driving seat was there, it wasn't in ALBSU. And then if you want to know why City and Guilds got involved it's because they were a vocational body and they were if you like the obvious ones, lots of things as far as the MSC, Training Agency (TA), Training , Education and Employment Development (TEED), and lots of the projects that we found ourselves doing around basic skills then were funded by one of the MSC successor bodies or another. (MG)

Our interviewees identified a number of reservations about Wordpower and Numberpower. These included concerns about a curriculum that was being driven by the awards, the level of understanding and knowledge that the assessment process was attempting to demonstrate, and the value of the award. Some argued it was about time that learners gained credit for their learning, and others were vehemently against the competence-based movement, upon which these qualifications were founded.

> At the point that they were introduced there was immense suspicion from the basic skills world of any concept of accreditation, and it was seen as introducing the possibility of failure, of destroying confidence rather than learning it. So then Wordpower and Numberpower were written explicitly to boost confidence and to address those concerns, they were written to be amenable to the evidence being created for individuals from the areas that they were motivated by; and they were written to be very practical and about the things learners would want and not the things that an employer would want. It was learner focused in that sense. (TF, Awarding Body)

The use of credit for learners continues to be hotly contested by tutors today and in many ways has been brought more sharply into focus through the creation of the national curriculum and testing within the *Skills for Life* strategy. Interestingly, the rationale for Wordpower and Numberpower can be contrasted directly with the current framework.

> We wanted something that was continuous accreditation and not a test. We wanted something at a number of levels so that people could take it and we wanted it to be broadly user friendly. (AW, BSA)

Proponents argued that tutors who really loved doing Wordpower and Numberpower did it creatively, and their students liked it too. Tutors describe a 'softly softly' approach to encouraging their learners to work towards a qualification, perhaps by offering it as a possibility, rather than a require- ment, often at the very first interview with a new learner. Wordpower and Numberpower could be used in different contexts, particularly in the work- place and through embedded basic skills, for example as part of a Good Hygiene Certificate. Detractors used strong language to describe their nega- tive views, from saying it was 'nit-picking', 'fundamentally misguided' and 'utterly loathsome', usually on the basis that the criteria did not reflect accurately what people needed to be able to do, or that account could be taken of people's 'spikey profiles' of differing ability in writing, reading and speaking within any level of the award. Again, RaPAL reported during this period on such views (see Herrington and Kendall, 2005).

The reluctance on the part of tutors and organisers to 'push' people into tak- ing qualifications is a tension to be managed when funding is partially depen- dent on the learners engaging with qualifications in basic skills.

> So if you were doing a basic skills class in literacy and numeracy you had to do Numberpower or Wordpower and the adults didn't want to do Number- power and Wordpower, they hated it. We didn't like delivering it and they didn't like doing it but that was the only way of getting funding through the local authority. (SM, London)

Notice how this respondent directly contradicts Alan Wells' claim that the learners liked it.

The slim evidence we have directly from learners (see Whitty, 1993), and from our own interviews with NCDS cohort members, indicates a broadly positive view and a clear appreciation of the differences between use and exchange value: that is, the value of certificates in validating learning and self-esteem as opposed to the instrumental value of having evidence to show employers and others, regardless of the real learning that has taken place.

Open College Network – an alternative framework

The first Open College began in the 1970s in the North West of England and quickly spread to all regions of the UK (Martin, 1988; Fieldhouse, 1996, p.74). In 1991 these local networks joined to form the National Open College Net- work (OCN) and, by the time the FEFC produced their inspection report in 1998, Open Colleges were becoming the main accrediting bodies for ALLN (see FEFC, 1998, p. 33). The Access movement had been established during this period, and the aim of the Open Colleges was to find an alternative means to accredit mature students, particularly those who did not have GCSE or 'A' Levels, but who wished to progress to further and higher education. In this respect, they function in the same way as the General Education Diploma (GED) in the US as an alternative means to gain entry to higher education (see Hillier, 1991). Open Colleges also provided an alternative framework to the NVQ system with which Wordpower and Numberpower were aligned. The OCN courses, although nationally accredited, were developed and delivered locally through regional networks, providing local responsiveness. It was perfectly possible to use this outcomes-based framework for foundation level study, i.e. basic literacy, numeracy and language.

One organiser who was seconded to work on the development of the Manchester Open College foundation level credits in basic skills described how this work helped him to reframe his views towards accreditation. He could see that basic skills could become part of a 'broader continuum of education provision'. The argument that people who already have qualifications should not stand in the way of those who don't was very powerful, countering some of the preciousness and protectiveness which people within the field felt.

The approach to develop Open College accreditation was based on an underlying philosophy that was completely student-centred in focus, but which took account of the need for quality assurance and accountability.

> ... it was important in terms of the ethos. It had to be sensitive, it had to be generated and focused very much on the learners' needs and experience but it also had to be rigorous, it had to be credible, and so that was a particular challenge. (JS, Manchester)

The OCN was not immune from the bureaucracy that any accredited system required. As the respondent above noted, the need to keep records 'caused complete consternation' in the field, at a time when practitioners and organisers lacked formal record keeping.

Progression

The underlying challenge throughout the development of assessment practices and accreditation frameworks for ALNE was how to establish progress. As we noted earlier, Deryn Holland's Progress Profiles attempted to enable learners to specify what they wanted to learn, how they were going to learn, what resources they required and how they knew they had been successful. Wordpower and Numberpower took this one stage further, by specifying precise activities and outcomes which could relate to the more generic competence-based approach underpinning most vocational qualifications during the 1990s. Articulation between qualifications, accreditation of prior experience and learning (APEL) and the identification of what, exactly, a qualification entitled someone to claim, in terms of their knowledge, skill and understanding, is an ongoing challenge, particularly in light of the status of academic versus vocational awards (see for example, Hodgson and Spours, 1997; Tomlinson, 2004). OCN had gone a long way to help specify progress with its hierarchy and progress paths, and its credit framework was the foundation for the later work of Hodgson, Spours, and Tomlinson. In Scotland, this framework was introduced in 1998, aligning its vocational and academic qualifications from compulsory education onwards (Raffe, 1997). Interestingly, as we noted in Chapter Eight, the qualifications used in ESOL have only just been brought into line with the *Skills for Life* curriculum and qualification framework having a more sophisticated qualification structure which is internationally recognised through the International English Language Testing Scheme (IELTS) and other awards for EFL.

Tensions and debates

Policy formation and implementation for assessment and accreditation in ALNE has been part of the move towards accountability, but has also been influenced by the wider competence-based movement adopted by the government from 1981 onwards, aiming to rationalise qualifications in the post-school sector. Moser reviewed the effectiveness of developments in assessment and accreditation in 1999 and the creation of *Skills for Life* was a direct consequence of his evaluation of the perceived lack of effectiveness of previous accreditation in the field. We can see that the problem of how learning can be measured has been stabilised through the use of accreditation and, latterly, testing. However, as our DPA would predict, we have uncovered numerous tensions which arise from the differing perspectives and voices of our heterogenous actors at national, regional and local levels. Below we provide an analysis of these perspectives, and link them to the wider context of how ALNE accreditation fits within a larger educational project of providing outcomes which enable economic success through the raised skill levels in the working population.

What learners want

Throughout the history of accreditation for basic skills, there has been a difference of opinion at to whether certain qualifications are appropriate for the learners. The tutors and the learners have held opposing views and these views have occasionally erupted into volatile confrontations. In one community-run scheme, local black people accused the organisers of being patronising by not working towards the standard GCSEs. A practitioner working at this programme at the time recalls:

> What we want is GCSEs, what this community needs is GCSEs and you are offering us just basic education presumably you think because that's all that black people are fit for'. And we had to stand up in that room and defend what we believed, and also hearing what they were saying, so it was a very, very powerful experience. (AH, London)

The value of any basic skills accreditation
The early days of resistance to credit may have been overcome for tutors but also the learners.

> ... from the first [OCN credit] in Manchester probably awarded in 1983, it's grown and the movement now has over half a million learners annually so it's interesting ... It was recognition for people who'd never had recognition before, but also for instrumental purposes to aid confidence-building and actual progression. One of the key questions in the early submission forms was 'What opportunities are there for progression?' What comes next? (JS, Manchester)

However, there is a problem with the status of a basic skills qualification, particularly for job seekers and those wishing to progress to further programmes of learning. A qualification carrying a title of basic skills labels the user as having low basic skills rather than as having improved them.

> Why would I need a qualification to tell everybody that I can't read and write?

> ... If you write down I have got [a qualification]in literacy or ESOL, the person reading it immediately knows that at one stage in your life you didn't know how to do these things. Whereas if you just fill in the form nicely and leave that piece off people can just see that you can read and write. (AZ, London)

Moser and beyond
We have noted earlier that the impetus of international attempts to address literacy and numeracy led to the setting up of Moser's committee in 1999. The arguments about the way in which each country could be rank ordered according to the results of IALS have been the subject of academic analysis (see Feinstein, 2003; Lavender et al, 2004). Its impact, then, across OECD countries has been profound. In England, the manifestation of government action has been to develop a new accreditation system, based firmly on the use of external testing which would use the existing item bank of questions

developed for a linked area, Key Skills. This decision once again demonstrates the permeability of policymaking, where a system is transferred to a parallel domain on the grounds that it is likely to be robust enough to work in the new context. However, not everyone on the committee agreed with Moser's resultant strategy, as one participant argued:

> You know from day one we argued about tests and qualifications. I believed very strongly that students need to assess their own learning and they need teachers to tell them where they are up to, that's absolutely bottom line. ... What learners want is the same qualification as everybody else. (AZ, London)

We found that interviewees wanted to discuss the current curriculum and testing regime, and its strengths and weaknesses. As we noted earlier, testing is highly controversial in terms of its validity as a means to establish learners' achievement. The current regime is particularly criticised with its emphasis on reading, rather than writing, to establish that someone has a certain level of literacy (see Mace, 2002; Mace, 1992).

> There is a modern irony of course which is that the national tests, which I would say I support, have nevertheless required people to do no writing whatsoever. (JP, London)

Furthermore, testing is used as a means to meet targets and, as Alan Wells argued, 'if you attach targets you encourage fiddling', maintaining that he has never been in favour of single tests, and that continuous assessment provides a better indication of people's knowledge and skill. The *Skills for Life* system, then, has exploded the underlying tensions we have identified in assessment, because provision is strictly controlled through funding, attached to targets and outcomes, and permitted only if it offers certain prescribed curriculum. The field has moved a long way from the informal interviews, flexible programmes and voluntary nature of working towards qualifications of the 1970s.

A wider context

We have shown that accreditation is a highly contested area of ALNE. This was not the only field of education from the beginning in which assessment has been subject to debate. Vocational education had long been associated with accreditation, but employers and businesses were not always sure of the ability of education and training to provide them with people who had the necessary knowledge and skills to work in the labour market. Criticisms of the ineffectiveness of vocational education and training (VET) became acute during the years of high unemployment and, to this effect, the White Paper on

Education and Training (1981) proposed a new council, the National Council for Vocational Qualifications, NCVQ, to oversee the creation of vocational qualifications which became known as the National Vocational Qualifications Framework, NVQF. The United Kingdom was not alone in its concern to produce qualified workers who would successfully contribute to the country's economy. European debate about up-skilling the workforce was also addressing the problems of high unemployment, particularly among young people, amid a growing backdrop of increasing use of technology and fears that countries outside Europe would become more highly competitive. The increasing interest of OECD in VET can be seen through its publications and research during this time (OECD, 1995, Gray and Griffin, 2000).

And for the future?

We have learnt lessons, which are being used in the new regime. Testing and assessment is at its best when it is done gently, to encourage people and identify their achievements. Yet accreditation can become an obsession which dominates practitioners' energy. There is a danger of teaching to the test. The awareness that there is greater focus and clarity with the current curriculum and qualification structure, coupled with significant resources, leads to lots of compromises (Lavender *et al*, 2004). The current *Skills for Life* strategy relies heavily on accreditation for both staff and learners. The on-going debate about the value of accreditation, and how best to represent the diverse needs of adults who wish to improve their basic skills, carries over into how practitioners should work within a curriculum which can only lead to credit.

> When I came back to basic education in 1994 I was really aware of how the teaching, the teachers were different, they had a different attitude ... by then we had to have accreditation, it was a good thing, the students wanted it, we were beginning to realise that we should think about progression and pro-gress and measuring distance of travel. What I realised was that teachers had become almost acclimatised, almost habituated to accreditation and there was a danger in that and there still is a danger in that ... I do think in the 1970s and 1980s we tended to work for ourselves and for our own plea-sure rather than for the student. (JD, London)

The spaces available to practitioners and learners to acknowledge the acquisition of literacy, numeracy and language have become more defined and controlled during the past thirty years. There are opportunities to learn outside the highly regulated system in England, but the lack of funding, in particular, makes it hard for more formal sites of learning (further education, adult and community learning, work-based learning) to provide a learning environment which does not require testing and working towards national qualifications. This space, then, is ripe for deliberative and reflexive action, and beginning to occur through, for example, editorials in the BSA newsletter. It remains to be seen if others will choose to join the ongoing quest to find appropriate ways to enable people to identify how much progress they have made, including, of course, gaining qualifications and other forms of credit.

10

Getting the message across: publicity and recruitment

... when the *On The Move* leaflets came out, I remember crossing by where there used to be education offices and I got this pile of leaflets about this high and you get a wind tunnel there. And this wind came out of the blue in a gust and blew the complete lot and they went in a spiral like a cyclone, right up into the air. Thousands of them, I lost the lot, and they came down like confetti over the whole of Leicester. Stood there, I've never been so embarrassed in my life. But publicity wise it was probably the most effective thing I could have done [laughs]. There were several thousand leaflets that just went up and drifted down. (AR, Practitioner, Leicester,)

... it is quite eerie how if the little piece of ... testimony came from a grandmother from Liverpool, amongst the phone calls received that very night were an extraordinarily high proportion of grandmothers from Merseyside, and you can almost play tunes on what happened ... so the lesson that I derived from that which ... I must say has informed everything I have since done in the field of broadcasting in Adult Education, is that what people respond to most is seeing someone who they perceive as being like them. (DH, BBC broadcaster)

Section 1: Introduction

In this chapter we will look both at the mass media campaigns that have been a recurrent feature of ALLN and at the local strategies used by practitioners, and hear people's views about the relative effectiveness of these. As authors, we both remember the early publicity campaign, and have subsequently used a variety of means to attract learners. Below, Mary recalls a recent experience which brings to the fore many of the challenges of attracting learners who were not easy to find, or encourage into ALLN provision.

> In 2003 I visited a beautiful coastal village in the remote far North West of England. Strolling through the middle of the village I noticed an old sticker in the corner of the window of the community centre. Half rubbed away and overlaid with grime it gave every appearance of belonging to a by-gone age but I recognised the logo and the message: 'For help with reading and writing phone this number'. (MH, Lancaster)

Designing publicity and recruitment for ALLN has always been a challenge for literacy-dependent educators. How can you communicate persuasively with people who can't, won't or don't access the written word in printed leaflets or ads? How can you best make use of people's everyday networks of friends and family who do access these and pass on the information by word of mouth?

As one solution to this challenge, the referral hotline, still used in media campaigns, was a revolutionary idea when it was invented by the BBC for the *On The Move* campaign back in 1975. Jenny Stephens, who worked for the BBC at the time, recalls:

> We had made what really was an apocalyptic decision to put a telephone number at the end of the programmes ... Nowadays, telephone help lines are two a penny but it had never been done before. The whole idea of the BBC campaign initially was to bring people forward and put them in touch with help, to motivate them, and to let them know that they weren't on their own. (JS, BBC Development Officer)

One of the unique aspects of the history of ALLN in the UK has been its close and creative relationship with the mass media and its careful attention to issues of publicity and recruitment. Before the literacy campaign in the mid-1970s, there had been occasional one-off newspaper articles and television coverage on the subject of adults, reading and writing. The television series *On the Move*, starring Bob Hoskins, was developed and produced by David Hargreaves, working with the Continuing Education Department of the BBC in partnership with voluntary organisations that were to mount the political campaign itself. Programmes were shown at Sunday teatime with daytime repeats. A parallel set of radio programmes aimed to recruit volunteer tutors. By December of 1975, 10,000 people had contacted the national helpline and this figure rose to 50,000 by the end of 1978. By 1978, 20,500 (Hargreaves, 1980: 51) volunteers had been trained to take part in the adult literacy campaign from national referrals. Many worked on a one-to-one basis in the home.

The involvement of the mass media in the field of ALLN is important for at least two reasons. Firstly, as in other fields of social policy, the mass media play a significant role in framing educational policy issues and promoting public awareness and debate. If we are right in seeing ALLN as a field of social policy that has effectively been created from scratch since the 1970s, then the role of the media in this process takes on special significance. Of particular interest are the ways in which images of the learners and teachers are constructed in media messages, how the teaching-learning process is represented and how the goals of adult literacy are articulated. Since illiteracy has frequently been perceived as a stigmatised state, presenting positive images of potential learners and breaking down negative stereotypes has always been a challenge for those creating publicity in the field. In our project, we gained access to some accounts of the debates around this that have taken place within media organisations themselves as well as among practitioners and policy actors.

Secondly, the mass media have always been seen as having a particularly strong and innovative role to play within the history of adult literacy, numeracy and ESOL because of the need to find alternative ways of communicating with people who cannot easily access the printed word.

There was an intention in the original adult literacy campaign to use the broadcast media to teach adult literacy through the programmes themselves. This has largely been forgotten except by those who developed the programmes and with it launched the new field of adult literacy. These developments did not take place in a vacuum, but came out of wider concerns and innovations of the time, including the introduction of the Open University in 1969 and optimism about the possible role of public and educational broadcasting in widening access to education (Hargreaves, 1980; Robinson, 1983; Sargant and Tuckett, 1997).

Such strategies generate a different order of response from the alternative word-of-mouth local outreach and marketing. Their very effectiveness brings its own problems. A constant theme for both policy actors and practitioners across the years has been that of how to balance the supply of suitable tutors and opportunities for learning with the demand from learners. The mass media have enormous power to raise public expectations that may be difficult to respond to since an infrastructure of trained support and facilities can only be built up gradually. Recurring questions faced by those organising publicity campaigns through the mass media include: Are enough resources allocated? Are practitioners supported enough? Are enough funds being directed into this area of work to enable the service to respond? In the 1970s, this was an urgent issue:

> ... if there was going to be enough provision, every single local authority in the country had to provide something and most of them were not. We knew that. So my job was to blackmail (they would say persuade but I would say blackmail) every single local education authority in the country to do something to set up tuition. At the time there were 125 of them in the UK and they were all totally independent. Each one had to agree to do something. (JS, BBC Development Officer)

Before the national media promoted the issue of adult literacy, schemes had developed around the country in a piecemeal way, through individual practitioners discovering a demand that had no name. A practitioner already working on a pioneering adult literacy programme with apprentices in an FE College in outer London recalls:

> We put a little bit in the local paper and it was May [1974] and when J. came home on half term he said what are we going to do? There have been 50 people ringing up! What? There can't be 50 people out there! This is before *On the Move* ... The Chief Education Officer was quoted in the paper as saying 'We don't have a literacy problem round here. At least, I have never met anyone who can't read and write'. At this point this tiny line in the local paper was producing all these enquiries. (GL, FE practitioner, London)

Media campaigns may build on work that is already going on, encouraging more local, regional and national co-ordination, and making the issues and the people involved more visible, affording them the recognition they deserve. They can also stimulate interest and activity in new areas as in the case of the original *On the Move* campaign. All the evidence from the 1970s clearly shows that most practitioners were starting from scratch in terms of training, teaching materials and resources. Although there was expertise in voluntary organisations, especially in the field of ESOL, provision was ad hoc and practitioners were isolated. One interviewee talked about having set something up in her living room to deal with the demand. Another interviewee, a practitioner at the time, described her experience in Liverpool. She received a consultation document about the programme that developed into *On the Move* (see *An outline of the contribution broadcasting might make to reducing adult illiteracy in the UK* – unattributed, undated BBC discussion paper circulated to LEAs and others in preparation for *On the Move* in Changing Faces archive) and also a phone call from the new national Adult Literacy Resource Agency (ALRA) asking whether she was ready to meet the demand.

> We are expecting a huge response, can you cope? People responded: I don't know whether I can cope or not, but we should take it anyway ... we'll have to develop systems that result from that. It was a wake-up call, there was going to have to be more provision because there would be huge demand through the broadcasts. (SG, practitioner, Liverpool)

Over the years the BBC campaigns were considered to be too successful and agencies could not cope with the demands. In his interview, David Hargreaves suggested that this was the issue that eventually slowed down the national media campaign, replacing it with more limited and carefully targeted local publicity.

> They started to say 'look, we shouldn't simply go on like this. This ... national broadcasting is a blunt instrument. It pulls forth demand where there is no supply ... this is getting to the point where it's counterproductive. You should back off from national broadcasting and you should ... do it on a much small scale, probably on radio ... and it should be regionalised. (DH, BBC broadcaster)

Later programmes had to be geared to developments in the field of policy and practice, rather than initiating them – a change in the power relations between the media and the policy makers. When the BBC become involved with promoting a major accreditation initiative, there were tensions between the three players, as one interviewee commented:

> ... the tension was that the producers were then told by the ALBSU ... look you've got to show how this links to Wordpower and Numberpower because this is linked to the accreditation initiative – all right! (PH, practitioner, London)

The thrust of the current *Skills for Life* policy initiatives is that many of the adults most in need of basic skills help will be difficult to reach and that it will be important to drive up demand for courses. This seems to be in contradiction to the experience of past media campaigns (as in the quote from David Hargreaves at the start of this chapter) where the response was often perceived or feared to overwhelm available provision and publicity needed to be fine-tuned to appeal to particular target groups that the government wanted to reach. The *Get On!* campaign, featuring the Gremlins, started after 2000 when our research was under way, but so many people mentioned it that we include discussion of this campaign later in this chapter. We specifically asked people from the NCDS survey about it, giving us a rare glimpse of potential learner perspectives.

Section 2: How the mass media have been used since the 1970's

We asked the people if they remembered *On the Move* and showed them stills from the early campaigns. Some recognised the logo: a simple outline drawing of the head and shoulders of a person holding an open book. Some recalled the BBC book with the green cover that had been just about the only teaching resource that tutors had at the time. People recognised the well-known British celebrity, Bob Hoskins, who started his career with this campaign. He played the everyman character, the street-wise lorry driver who couldn't spell. People we spoke to were amazed to see pictures of him with hair ... 'bloody hell, yes, Bob Hoskins!'

The most popular programmes remembered without prompting in both individual and group interviews were *On the Move* and *Parosi*. Typically practitioners remembered (or had heard about) *On the Move*. They remembered the names of a few campaigns most closely related to their own work, and then the most recent *Get On!* campaign about which people held strong opinions. Individuals who were directly consulted or involved in the making of programmes tended to have more detailed memories of those. Practitioners remembered seeing the early pilots that were trialled around the country as well as the panic of reacting to the new demand. Individual practitioners, however, either those presently working or those who had retired, were not necessarily able to judge the general impact of media campaigns and their value and were vague about numbers who had been referred, or whether indeed the campaigns had had any lasting impact as compared with the word of mouth and continual local outreach strategies that they relied on.

Over the years, media campaigns have been carried by adverts, storylines in popular soaps (such as Channel 4's *Brookside* in the 1990s which was accompanied by teaching materials accessed in local schemes via the *learndirect* phone line); specially created educational programmes, news items and documentaries. The original *On the Move* series was clearly a campaign because it was tied to a policy agenda and was explicitly trying to rally support, both from volunteers and potential learners. Similarly, *Step Up to Wordpower* at the end of the 1980s was an integrated part of a new policy initiative to introduce accreditation to literacy programmes. *The National Year of Reading* in 1998 and the Get-On campaign featuring the Gremlin characters and associated with the *Skills for Life* policy are other clear-cut cases, but there have been many media initiatives whose origins and intentions are less clear. For example, documentary programmes such as those shown periodically by *World in Action* or *Dispatches* can be very influential in shaping public perceptions of literacy issues, but may be isolated programmes with no follow up or co-ordination with policy. *Liberating Literacy* that featured members of the Pecket Well College, women's groups during the miner's strike and other radical initiatives were clearly putting over an empowering image of the possibilities of literacy programmes, but not necessarily a representative view of what was happening in the field at the time. Other programmes such as *Parosi* (Neighbours) or the family literacy initiative *Read and Write Together* were offered more as direct teaching/learning resources than having a campaigning orientation.

Regular representations of literacy, numeracy and ESOL appear incidentally in newspaper and television coverage and may unintentionally promote existing stereotypes and perhaps run counter to the deliberate campaigning messages. For example, an episode of *Brookside* that ran alongside the positive campaign featured a character experiencing difficulties with an uncaring and bureaucratic FE college.

When *On the Move* was mentioned this was remembered more in terms of raising awareness, challenging and overcoming the stigma of illiteracy. In terms of awareness and motivation, the campaign made its mark on the general public and attracted volunteers, such as these interviewees who wanted to get involved in this area of work where they have remained to this day:

> I watched it on TV, I never missed it, fascinating programme it was only 10 minutes but it was really good … I could read and write but I just watched it as entertainment and it did change perception, there is no getting away from it. (AP, practitioner, London)

> I got involved because there was, well first of all I was at home, I was a mother and young child and I used to watch the *On the Move* programme on the TV. I was absolutely enthralled by it all and just had a fancy that I could get involved. (MC, practitioner, London)

Parosi tended only to be recalled by people active in the ESOL movement. Its impact was felt more in areas of the country where there were high concentrations of ethnic minorities at the time, such as Birmingham, Coventry and London. Some ESOL practitioners interviewed have mentioned *Parosi's* impact on the Local Authority funding of home tutor schemes. In other areas of the country, the needs of these groups were not considered to be important. For example, one of our more rural case study areas, Norfolk, had very little ESOL during the 1970s and 1980s; apart from the Vietnamese boat people few ethnic minorities arrived in Norfolk. This has now changed due to more recent policies of dispersing refugees around the country.

As for numeracy campaigns, with prompting we have found some awareness of the *Count Me In* campaign by the BBC. This seems to be the one best re-membered over the decades. The use of celebrities in these programmes clearly affects people's memories. For example, one London-based inter-viewee commented:

> That was Carol Voderman, was it Carol Voderman? ... I remember their names but I don't actually remember what they looked like and what they did ... they obviously didn't make a major impact on me did they? (JR, prac-titioner, London)

The *National Year of Reading* in 1998, launched by an enthusiastic New Labour government, is perhaps the most co-ordinated media literacy cam-paign to date. A broad range of media messages were used, from advertise-ments to soap-lines in *EastEnders* and *Brookside*. There were newspaper articles and posters, featuring footballers who were pictured grinning be-tween goal posts and displaying children's books. National and local papers ran stories of reading marathons and literacy awards. News International promoted *Free Books for Schools* through the *Sun* and the *Times*, encouraging school children and their teachers to collect the tokens on packets of Walkers crisps to exchange for books. The headmistress of one primary school dressed up as a giant crisp packet in order to promote her family-fun-readathon in the local press.

Since 2001, the *Get On!* campaign has been running as part of the English *Skills for Life* strategy. This time the heroes are not the friendly everyman figures like Bob Hoskins, but the Gremlins, unpleasant and ugly characters intended to externalise people's fears of literacy and numeracy problems (see Barnes, 2005). As well as television peak-time advertisements on ITV and Channel 4, the Gremlins, like all good tie-in campaigns, also feature on a range of merchandise: beer mats, advertisements on bus stops, post-cards, bus tickets, desk calendars, radio advertisements, people dressing up as giant gremlins for local photo opportunities and a range of other publicity. Parallel campaigns in Wales and Scotland have their own separately designed broad-casts. The use of helplines and referral services has now been linked into the promise of a whole world of on-line learning through *learndirect*, in line with current excitement about the possibilities of new Information and Com-munications Technologies (ICTs). The scale of response to the *Get On!* cam-paign is of a different order from *On the Move*. The DfES in 2005 reported

350,000 calls to *learndirect* compared to the 50,000 referrals that David Hargreaves reported for the period 1975-78.

However, such highly co-ordinated campaigns are expensive and time-consuming. Without proper planning, things can fall apart: for example, in the *Count Me In!* programmes there were technical difficulties with the accompanying CD Rom which may have led to the project not being as successful as initially anticipated. And it is not just adults in need of help with basic skills who watch, respond, are exposed to publicity or identify with the characters in the programmes. The general public is also affected: attitudes are changed and awareness is raised. Within the general public are other groups: parents, teachers, potential volunteers, children, employers and different groups respond differently, reflecting their particular orientation to the issue of adult literacy.

We asked the 78 people from the NCDS interviewed as part of the *Changing Faces* project to comment on a range of advertising for ALLN since the 1970s, including the Gremlins. Though most recognised the Gremlin figures, they were not always clear what the campaign had been about. Even those who did get the message did not see the publicity as targeted at them. From the distantly remembered *On the Move* to the current Gremlins campaign, people felt that ALLN would be good for people who need it, but did not count themselves as being in that group, even though we had chosen them carefully as people whose profiles fitted the current government target group. Several had phoned the helpline on behalf of others. Two had phoned on their own account and one of these had enrolled on a course as a result. The other had been turned away as having problems with spelling that could not be catered for within the local programme.

Section 3 'Get down to the baby clinic': the role of outreach in ALLN

> Since we opened in 1991, we have never advertised for students. When we started we put leaflets up obviously but since 1992 we have done very little advertising. We get a mention in the college prospectus because we have to be there but we have never advertised. It is all word of mouth or people just walking past and seeing what is on the window. So it is more of people get to know us and tell their friends or their family rather than us actually actively going out and getting people in. (CW, practitioner, Leics)

The importance and skill of outreach workers echoes throughout our data but funders and policy-makers have found it hard to build in these activities adequately to ALLN services. We now have learning champions and union learning reps but when ALLN moved in the FE colleges, as Alan Wells admits, outreach work did not fit the institutional job categories and got seriously squeezed out:

> ... the nature of colleges is they are a big ship that's difficult to change. The worst they did do things like ... you have got an engineering lecturer who has got a few spare hours couldn't he do basic skills, you don't need to do all that outreach, its expensive. Colleges were being squeezed themselves so running outreach centres or things like that was not a good idea when you were going to be paid for how good it was. (AW, BSA, London)

Outreach involved a variety of activities, including visiting people in their own homes.

> What they used to do is give us these sheets of yellow paper with names and addresses on and people who are interested and we had to go around their houses! Can you imagine we used to send people out knocking on doors! On their own! (JW, practitioner, Manchester)

Limitations on word of mouth, though, were pointed out by an FEU research report reviewing adult education provision in Sheffield (an LEA with progressive equal opportunities policies) that included ESOL and linked skills classes. After showing in detail the ethnocentrism of the printed publicity, the authors of the report go on to comment:

> Interviews with students and the community reveal that much reliance is placed upon word of mouth. Although this can be effective, there are inherent dangers ... relying on word of mouth publicity simply reinforces the social composition of existing students. If the Black communities are underrepresented or if certain groups (e.g. Bengali) are apparently excluded, the danger is that word of mouth publicity will not reach them. Direct publicity through community grapevines is very important in closely knit communities. (FEU, 1989 p 7-8)

Assessing the impact of publicity campaigns:

Apart from the meticulous evidence assembled by David Hargreaves in his 1980 book about *On the Move*, there is little data in the public domain about the impact of media campaigns. The most common monitoring activity associated with media campaigns is to estimate numbers watching programmes via audience panel surveys, and to report the numbers using referral hotlines as a gauge of public response. Much of this evidence is collected by broadcasters themselves. Audience response studies are a form of market research survey, used developmentally so the findings are not in the public domain.

We spoke to several people involved with producing programmes, who had access to the figures, as insiders: For example, Pat Hulin had access to figures for the *Stepping Up* Programmes when she worked for the BBC, but these were not in the public domain, Naomi Sargant, who has worked for Channel 4, similarly had figures. There are summary figures only available from the current *Get On!* campaign, showing that around 350,000 people have called the hotline since 2001, and 23 per cent of those who call the phone-line take up learning opportunities (DfES, 2005). Beyond this basic monitoring exercise, little effort appears to have been made to pursue the research opportunity offered by this surge of interest and find out in more detail who the callers are and where they end up.

Section 4: Issues and debates emerging across the whole period

The use of the mass media to raise public awareness and recruit students is a unique part of the story of ALLN in the UK. We have shown here how the mass media have been used throughout as a significant complement to local 'word of mouth' recruitment activities and have played a key role in shaping public understandings of the issues and image of the learner. As in the original *Right to Read* campaign, *Skills for Life* has used media promotion as a key part of its strategy.

The *On the Move* campaign used an 'everyman' character to invite people to identify and emphasised the right to educational opportunity. The *Get On!* campaign assumes different motivations and reluctance to take up learning and thus takes a more aggressive approach. The changing discourses of government policy in this area, especially the promotion of a marketing discourse, are reflected in changing media strategies. The organisation of media institutions has also changed significantly since the 1970s (see Goodwin, 1998). The ethos of public broadcasting and the debates surrounding it have significantly shifted and all channels now operate in a more or less protected commercial environment. Mass media public education campaigns have increasingly taken on the characteristics of advertising and the *Get On!* campaign was devised not in-house by a BBC producer but by an independent producer in the shape of an advertising campaign. As in all good advertising, the campaign includes tie ins such as beer mats and desk calendars, the co-ordination of multiple media, and ways of prompting the audience to respond directly in order to buy into the product on offer. This a strategy into which the original broadcasting support services fit well.

Likewise, the notion of outreach workers, networking on their patch, common in the early days, gave way to marketing as the culture changed in parallel ways in the education and training area more generally. The evidence from our interviews suggests that the twin strategies of outreach into communities alongside informal word of mouth publicity via trusted referral points are still seen as key to recruitment by many practitioners. There is much less agreement amongst practitioners about the real payoff of many mass campaigns, though none of the policy actors really questioned this.

Change agency in the development of ALLN was originally strongly located in the BBC and in the voluntary organisations rather than government or existing adult education establishments and the LEAs who are presented as being dragged along with the campaign, more or less willingly. The catalytic role of the state-funded BBC with its close relationship to the political establishment of the time is intriguing. Once ALBSU was established it took over, directing more limited and carefully targeted programmes and campaigns, for example Wordpower and Numberpower, in partnership with the BBC but very closely responding to government policy and pressures around accountability and assessment. In the 1990s, research was a trigger for change, strongly promoted by the BSA, and OECD research was used as a rationale for *Skills for Life*. The media campaign was set up after the government strategy had been settled.

Right from the start of the *On the Move* campaign tensions emerged from the challenge of needing more services in place to meet the anticipated increase in demand. Similar tensions are re-surfacing now with the sudden policy and media activity of the *Skills for Life* campaign. The views of broadcasters and educationalists about learners and the nature and institutional frameworks necessary for learning to take place are reflected in debates about whether programmes are designed to recruit or to teach.

Throughout the period we have studied, practitioners and students have been approached by media programme makers to furnish examples of programmes, profiles of typical students or good quotes but rarely to shape the programmes themselves and their messages. Apart from some involvement in piloting programmes, the deliberative space for practitioners and learners has remained at the level of local and informal discussions. When consulted they are, however, articulate and interested in these recruitment issues which are central to practicing and accessing learning ALLN.

All the way through this period, practitioners and learners have also made use of the media to lobby for funds and to put over their perspective on ALLN.

The Friends Centre Teach-in in 1981, organised to protest against reductions in funding for adult education, illustrates the range of strategies people have used. The list of press coverage for this event included feature articles, photos and letters in local and national, popular and serious papers. Interviews were given on TV and radio news programmes, there was live coverage on local radio and spots on a range of national programmes from John Peel's music programme, to *Woman's Hour.*

11

Conclusion: making changes

We have proposed a view of social policy that focuses on the everyday practices and realities of those affected by it. We have seen that most of the adults who are the focus of ALLN policy and practice have never taken part formally in lifelong learning. ALLN is faced, therefore, with the dual task of advocating for better access for these people to formal learning and, equally important, supporting them outside education in their purposes for literacy and numeracy. We have seen that practitioners, highly skilled in the practical tactics of working within marginal spaces and strongly imbued with an inheritance of volunteerism, still invoke the ideal of student-centred learning. We have seen policy actors, working from a range of institutional positions, searching for ways of making ALLN tractable as a policy problem that can be solved, looking for a 'workable definition of the problem or a temporary stabilisation' (Hajer and Wagenaar, 2003: 23). Reaching such a temporary stabilisation was a consistent aim of the national agency for ALLN throughout the period we have examined, as it attempted to hold open a space for the newly developing field to emerge.

In locating ALLN within the bigger policy landscape, we have seen how the era of welfare rights which inspired the original literacy campaign was already passing by the time ALLN had become established. Assumptions about the balance of rights and obligations between individual and the state has changed. We have described the interplay between several agendas. There are long-standing ideological divisions and debates about the value of academic versus vocational education and training; the relative importance of lifelong learning and initial education; how to deal with difference and diversity in education; what counts as 'proper English' and how this is implicated in distinctions of ethnicity, social class and nationhood. Societal views of the rights and obligations of citizenship are reflected and modelled within the learning polity through compulsory or voluntary participation in learning and through the democratic or hierarchical practices and social relations created within learning programmes.

The need to manage the tensions thrown up by competing visions within the field, and changing priorities in wider social policy, contribute to the precariousness of policy solutions and can result in ambiguous and contradictory decisions and initiatives.

Learning from a deliberative policy analysis
1. Chronology
From timelines of key moments and events, we have identified four major phases in ALLN since the early 1970s, documenting the steps along the way that have led to the present *Skills for Life* strategy. They reveal times of national policy absence, of lacunae, where change was caused by other social policies. These policies impacted on ALLN, for good or ill, in unintended ways that had to be managed and accommodated. The confused diversity of funding sources resulting from ALLN's placement within this tangle of policy interests has particularly shaped and often constrained its development. The strategic vision and influence of both local authorities and national agencies has been key to how the field has been able to cope with these changes. Throughout, practitioners and policy activists at all levels continued to promote their work to affect the policymaking agenda.

2. Discourses
Our analysis shows how literacy and numeracy, learners, teachers, the learning process and the institutional context have been represented differently at different points in time. These representations have been shaped by bigger shifts in the way adults are viewed by social policy, as learners, consumers, as parents and as workers. They have also been heavily influenced by the mass media both through periodic interest in the news media linked to moral panics about educational standards and also through intentional campaigns, such as *On the Move, The National Year of Reading* and *Get On!* The role of the mass media in people's lives has changed significantly since the early 1970s and public education messages are received within an environment saturated with persuasive advertising.

At the beginning there was a lack of a coherent discourse in the field, and those mobilising around it drew on existing discourses rooted in earlier work and contributing fields such as remedial and primary education, community development and vocational further education. International influences included radical mass literacy campaigns and UNESCO's work on functional literacy. The prevalent view of learners was as illiterate and disadvantaged but deserving of a second chance in education. ESOL learners were seen through the conflicted lens of race relations and immigration policy.

Uneasiness about and constant changes of name for the field and its participants reflects the ideological divisions noted above, as well as the search for a non-discriminatory vocabulary for a stigmatised aspect of difference which is common to other areas of social policy and education (see Hevey, 1992). The national agency (now the BSA) played a key role in creating a normalised image of adult learners and in defining and policing the boundaries of the field. As a quasi-government agency, it advocated for the field through research, through use of the media and by responding to the policy mantras of the day to press the case for basic skills.

Despite this unified national voice, many differences exist among policy actors, practitioners and adult learners and there is a degree of awareness of the tensions and compromises that result from these differences. There are continuing debates about appropriate names for the field and about relationships between ESOL numeracy and literacy.

3. Change agents

We have argued that policy is constructed and enacted in local ways, not only by learners and practitioners but also by many national policy actors. We have identified the primary change forces that have been important influences at different points as the field developed. These are found during each of the four policy phases, and expressed through a variety of organisations and networks. Relationships between these changed, as different agencies rose and fell in prominence. Change agents are not just people or organisations. Events and ideas can become reified as myths that take on an agency of their own. Notions of a student writing movement or dyslexia are examples of this, as are estimates of need such as seven million adults.

There are clear examples of national policy impacting forcefully on local contexts and on individuals, especially in the late 1980s/early 1990s with introduction of a contract culture and incorporation of the further education colleges.

Many players in the story of ALLN have had multiple roles within a range of institutions, as practitioners also as lobbyists and decision-makers. Such individuals link different spheres of activity and can play particularly key roles in making changes.

We have collected many examples of campaigning and advocacy both inside and outside existing institutional structures involving stakeholder groups including trade unions, government based champions, practitioner and learner-led networks. These range from high profile, direct action in the form of locally organised protests against funding, pay and conditions, to the use of the parliamentary process through private members' bills, giving evidence to select committees, lobbying councillors and MPs. Much activism takes the form of mundane work within local networks, committees and governing bodies, pursuing funding to enable specific developments in practice and policy to take place.

Finally we have noted the role of the media and research communities as change forces. By 'change' people often mean observable differences in policy or practice. However, the changes in discourses we have discussed above are also at times an important result of sustained, deliberate work. Articulating new understandings of the field, compiling evidence and making space for testimonials from learners has been a crucial part of making change in ALLN.

Research evidence hardly existed at the start of the 1970s but quantitative estimates of need and benefit had become a major part of the policy rhetoric by the time of the Moser review. Many practitioners carried out small-scale research and documented their practice, with specific funding from national agencies, encouraged by professional development courses or associations like RaPAL and NATECLA.

4. Tensions

Historical study reveals ALLN to be a dynamic, heterogenous field, replete with myths, flashpoints and mantras. There are gaps between policy and practice in both national and local fields of action. The differing perspectives held by actors in the field, coupled with external factors outlined above, created a number of enduring tensions which have had to be managed by policy actors, practitioners and learners alike. We have tracked the way people have responded to these tensions, sometimes resisting and sometimes using strategic compliance in what has been described as 'local contentious practice' (Holland and Lave, 2001:7).

These tensions surface time and again and are expressed in a variety of ways, depending on the context. Tensions exist between practitioners in literacy, numeracy and ESOL; between private trainers and those working in college and community-based programmes. Workplaces, prisons, voluntary and statutory programmes all have their own ways of working.

Finally, there are the normalising and competitive pressures of international standards. The globalising goals of international agencies, mediated by national policy, impact on practice through performance indicators and the outcomes required by funding bodies. These governing influences come with their own discourses and social relations, re-organising teachers' (and managers') work and learners' experiences. The tension here is how to acknowledge and respond to diversity among learners whilst working within a mainstreamed, systematised field of provision. The *Skills for Life* strategy has normalised ALLN by introducing a national curriculum and a set of standards to which practitioners must aspire (see Fowler, 2004). The use of targets encourages strategic compliance and accreditation continues to be a source of tension, particularly the use of limited literacy tests that do not measure writing. Students who progress quickly attract more funding than those with more complex learning needs, thus skewing provision (Bathmaker, 2005).

5. Deliberative space

Public spaces for deliberative, reflexive communication amongst interested parties in ALLN surface only occasionally. They have been present by default in some local areas, through training and verifying networks of practitioners and, more structurally, through local authority-organised groups. But the deliberative policy stance articulated by Hajer and Wagenaar requires much more than this. It puts forward a radically altered conceptualisation of citizenship, politics and the state. It suggests that people should not only be included in the process of policy formulation, policy making and implementation, but that there should be a continuing search for appropriate ways to do so. The spirit of enquiry, then, requires an ongoing process of assessment of what is 'intense social interaction' (Hajer and Wagenaar, 2003:24), as well as the interaction between our knowledge and the concrete situation at hand.

People have told us stories which have helped them, and us, to 'shape, grasp and legitimate' the actions and the situations that gave rise to them (Hajer and Wagenaar, 2003: 156). We have identified, in these stories, where people's actions have been enabled through the structures and institutions that were in place before and during the creation of the ALLN field, where they have been consulted and included in committees and where information has been gathered from the actors in the field who have intimate experience of the practices of ALLN. We have identified spaces that individuals have carved out for themselves, perhaps through additional research or study, taking time to reflect and challenge their daily, taken for granted activities. Networks have grown, disintegrated and reappeared over time. These have provided opportunities to cross the practice-learner-policy divides.

We have also found frequent barriers, and a lack of space for action. It has been difficult for ALLN practitioners to consolidate their professional expertise and policy involvement. A lack of formal representative networks and associations and (until recently) training has meant that practitioners have only been able to make token contributions to new developments. The policy turn away from the use of volunteers has meant that ALLN has not fully developed the potential roles of the many individual volunteers who are still working in local programmes. Whilst national agencies like ALBSU did campaign on behalf of the field, they made little attempt to canvas opinion among practitioners or to develop policy forums. Their tactical manoeuvring on behalf of ALLN was therefore little understood. They were perceived by many practitioners as being remote and inaccessible and even to have sold out.

Where are we now? moving through the past and present to the future

Even with the unprecedented level of funding available through the *Skills For Life* strategy, ALLN continues to struggle to assert its legitimacy, to get across its messages about what works, and to claim both physical and metaphorical space in the post-compulsory education and training sector. ALLN has been damaged by accident before and could be so again as LSC money is cut back and colleges, desperate to balance their books, reduce the resources on which ALLN learners disproportionately depend.

As one of the few educational fields to have really grappled with issues of access for adult returning students, ALLN can claim a significant place within the larger history of the access movement, widening participation to FE and HE, community development and popular lifelong learning. Its specific contributions include showing how the mass media can be successfully used for recruitment, to widen participation among the large group of those still estimated to be in need, to change negative attitudes to learners and to raise public awareness of a social policy issue. It has paid careful attention to initial referral, induction and personalised mentoring; explored the possibilities of flexible delivery in terms of both time and place. It has achieved statutory status for funding and an entitlement to free courses. It has held tenaciously to the values of a student-centred curriculum and small group work within structures that made these increasingly difficult to achieve. It has experimented (imperfectly) with democratic learning processes and structures. It has drawn attention to the special powers of writing and maths to improve life chances and the exercise of citizenship. It has explored the effects of changing technologies on learning. In developing and testing strategies in these areas it has influenced a wider field.

The *Skills for Life* strategy has galvanised new energy and ideas and has been a serious attempt to embed ALLN within a state-funded system of learning opportunities. We predict that this temporary stabilisation of ALLN will move on. But whatever the official shape and name of the field in the future, activists will continue to advocate for it through ingenious everyday tactics. ALLN will continue to be entwined in the push and pull of surrounding social policy, with all the tensions and contradictions that this implies. Most importantly, the field will continue to change as new communication technologies, social and political events re-shape the everyday practices of language, literacy and numeracy.

Glossary

ABE	Adult Basic Education
ABSSU	Adult Basic Skills Strategy Unit
ACACE	Advisory Council for Adult and Continuing Education
ACE	Adult and Continuing Education
AE	Adult Education
ALBSU	Adult Literacy and Basic Skills Unit (later the BSA)
ALI	Adult Learning Inspectorate
ALLN	Adult Literacy, Language and Numeracy
ALM	Adults Learning Maths
ALNE	Adult Literacy, Numeracy and ESOL
ALRA	Adult Literacy Resource Agency (later the BSA)
ALU	Adult Literacy Unit (later the BSA)
BALID	British Association for Literacy in Development
BAS	British Association of Settlements
BBC	British Broadcasting Corporation
BSA	Basic Skills Agency
BSAI	Basic Skills Accreditation Initiative
C&G	City and Guilds (an awarding body)
CABSU	Central Area Basic Skills Unit (Manchester)
CRE	Commission for Racial Equality
CTAD	Cambridge Training and Development Ltd.
DES	Department of Education and Science
DfEE	Department for Education and Employment
DfES	Department for Education and Skills
DE	Department of Employment
DPA	Deliberative Policy Analysis
EARAC	East Anglian Regional Advisory Council
EFL	English as a Foreign Language
ESF	European Social Fund
ESOL	English for Speakers of Other Languages or English as a Second or Other Language

ESRC	Economic and Social Research Council
EU	European Union
FE	Further Education
FEDA	Further Education Development Agency
FEFC	Further Education Funding Council
FENTO	Further Education National Training Organisation
FEU	Further Education Unit (a development unit)
FHE	Further and Higher Education
FWWCP	Federation of Worker Writers and Community Publishers
GCSE	General Certificate of Secondary Education
GED	General Equivalency Diploma
GEST	Grant for Education to Support Teachers
HE	Higher Education
HMI	Her Majesty's Inspectors (of Education)
HMSO	Her Majesty's Stationery Office
IALS	International Adult Literacy Survey
ICT	Information and Communications Technologies
IELTS	International English Language Testing Scheme
ILEA	Inner London Education Authority
ILP	Individual Learning Plan
ILTU	Industrial Language Training Units
IMF	International Monetary Fund
ITC	Initial Teaching Certificate
LEA	Local Education Authorities
LLU	Language and Literacy Unit
LSC	Learning and Skills Council
LSDA	Learning and Skills Development Agency
LU	Lancaster University
MALEC	Manchester Adult Literacy Education Coalition
MSC	Manpower Services Commission
NACRO	National Association for the Care and Rehabilitation of Offenders
NATECLA	National Association for Teaching English and other Community Languages
NATFHE	National Association of Teachers in Further and Higher Education
NCDS	National Child Development Survey
NCVQ	National Council for Vocational Qualifications
NFER	National Foundation for Educational Research
NFVLS	National Federation of Voluntary Literacy Schemes
NGO	Non-governmental organisation
NIACE	National Institute for Adult and Continuing Education (formerly NIAE)
NLS	New Literacy Studies
NRDC	National Research and Development Centre (for Adult Literacy and Numeracy)

NSA	National Students' Association
NUPE	National Union of Public Employees
NVQ	National Vocational Qualification
NVQF	National Vocational Qualifications Framework
OCN	Open College Network
OECD	Organisation for Economic Cooperation and Development
Ofsted	Office for Standards in Education
OLC	Open Learning Centre
Q mark	Quality mark
RaPAL	Research and Practice in Adult Literacy
RDA	Regional Development Agency
RSA	Royal Society of Arts (an awarding body)
SK4L	Skills for Life
SLDD	Students with Special Learning Difficulties or Disabilities
TEC	Training and Enterprise Council
TOPS	Training Opportunities Programme
UNESCO	United Nations Educational, Social and Cultural Organisation
UNISON	The public service workers union was created in 1993 through the merger of Nalgo (National Association of Local Government Officers), COSHE (Confederation of Health Employees) and NUPE (National Union of Public Employees), the three unions traditionally representing Local Government, Health Authority and Nationalised Industry staff.
VET	Vocational Education and Training

YOPS Scheme – Youth Opportunities Scheme

YTS	Youth Training Scheme

Appendix 1: Timelines

	1970	1972	1974	1976
Policy Initiatives	♦ UNESCO *Experimental Literacy Programme*	♦ Russell Report ♦ BAS *Status Illiterate, Prospects Zero* ♦ Haviland Report		♦ Bullock ♦ MSC funds TO ♦ Callaghan's R Speech
Institutions		♦ MSC Created	♦ MSC ILTU formed	♦ LLU set up ♦ ALRA formed
Media Programmes			♦ *On the Move*	♦ *Parosi*
Professional Development				♦ BBC Tutor Ha and Student Wo ♦ NFVLS
Accreditation and Accountability				

8	1980	1982	1984
♦NUPE creates WORKBASE			♦Swann Report
YOPS	♦Creation of YTS		
		♦Cockcroft Report *Mathematics Counts*	
	♦ACACE Report: *A strategy for Adult Basic Education*		
	♦ALBSU created		
			♦ESOL added to ALBSU's remit
A becomes ALU			
k For Yourself			♦*Switch on to English*
e It Count			
			♦*Write Now*
♦*Cross talk*			
	♦ALBSU Regional Training Programme (until 1993)		♦RaPAL formed
ESLA formed			
Qualifications limited to RSA and City and Guilds, e.g. RSA's CCE			

	1986	1988	1990	1992
Policy Initiatives		♦ Education Reform Act		♦ FHE Act ♦ ALBSU Basic Skills a▮
Institutions		♦ ILEA abolished		♦ FEF▮
Media Programmes			♦ *Wordpower* and *Numberpower*	
Professional Development		♦ City and Guilds Qualifications introduce▮	♦ Adults Learning Math▮	
Accreditation and Accountability	♦ NCVQ formed	♦ ALBSU Progress Profile ♦ NFER Occupational Skills Test ♦ Training Agency review of Assessment T▮	♦ Open College Netwo▮ ♦ ALBSU Qua▮	

1994	1996	1998	2000
	◆ European Year of Lifelong Learning		◆ White Paper *Learning to Succeed*
		◆ National Literacy Strategy in Schools	
	◆ Tomlinson Report		◆ The Moser Report *A Fresh Start*
			◆ Learning Skills Council created
ed	◆ ALBSU becomes BSA		
			◆ *Skills for Life* strategy
		◆ National Year of Reading. Storylines in soaps *Brookie Basics* and *Eastenders*	
◆ *Family Learning*			
		◆ *Count Me In*	◆ DfES *Get On*
			◆ New Qualifications planned
		◆ FEFC Adult Basic Skills Inspection report	
rk	◆ OECD IALS		◆ ALI created
ues	◆ Qualifications and Curriculum Authority		

Appendix 2
List of Archival Sources for ALLN

Whilst we were researching the history of ALLN we discovered a number of useful archive resources. These are listed below for anyone interested in taking a deeper look at particular aspects of ALLN or related areas.

The Basic Skills Resource Centre, set up by the Basic Skills Agency in 1993 holds many of their publications: www.ioe.ac.uk/

British Association of Settlements and Social Action, the organization that initiated the original Right to Read Campaign: www.bassac.org.uk

Federation of Worker Writers and Community Publishers holds many student and working class publications from the 1980s onward: http://thefwwcp.org.uk

Archive of the Further Education Funding Council contains inspection reports and other publications from the 1990s: http://lsc.wwt.co.uk/documents

Mass Observation Archive founded in 1937 aimed to document everyday life in Britain through empirical observation, diaries, and photographs: www.massobs.org.uk

Manchester Archives and Local Studies include historical documents and photographs of education in Manchester: www.manchester.gov.uk/libraries/arls/

NATFHE Professional association for teachers in FE colleges and adult education from the 1980s to 2006: www.natfhe.org.uk

NIACE a well-organized collection of materials on adult education throughout the period. Includes documents from the ACACE and board meetings of ALBSU: www.niace.org.uk

Oral History Society Information about oral history methodology and collections: www.oralhistory.org.uk

The Ruskin Library, Oxford University holds the *Write First Time* archive, and includes information about the NFVLS and the NSA:. www.lancs.ac.uk/users/ruskinlib/

Source for historical documents about London Includes The Trades Union Congress Library, and the Workers Educational Association National archive: www.londonmet.ac.uk/services/sas/library-services/tuc/

Sources for history of women and education: www.thewomenslibrary.ac.uk
www.genesis.ac.uk

General Catalogues describing archives held throughout England and dating
from the 900s to the present day: http://www.archiveshub.ac.uk www.a2a.org.uk

UK Data Archives holding on-line research resources in the form of both
qualitative and numerical data: www.data-archive.ac.uk http://www.esds.ac.uk

The National Archives: http://www.pro.gov.uk/

The British Library, including Colindale newspaper library: http://www.bl.uk/

UNESCO historical archive of international literacy initiatives:
www.unesco.org/education/uie/documentation

Appendix 3: List of Interviewees Quoted

The following people have given permission for their names to be attributed to quotes in this book

Sylvia Benterman, Norfolk
Jean Brown, Leics
Sue Cara, Norfolk
Helen Casey, London
Joy Chapman, Leics
Mariette Clare, Leics
Julia Clarke, London
Carol Crompton, Manchester
Michael Crook, Norfolk
Jay Derrick, London
Sue Edge, Manchester
Judith Edwards, Manchester
Maggie Evans, London
Stella Fitzpatrick, Manchester
Roy Flude, Leics
Tony Forster, London
Sue Gardener, London
Judith Gawn, London
David Gibson, Manchester
Bernard Godding, Norfolk
David Hargreaves, BBC
Roxy Harris, London
Lindsey Hartford, Manchester
Margaret Herrington, Leics
Ursula Howard, now NRDC
Pat Hulin, London
Sue Jepson, Manchester
Jane Jordan, Manchester
Chris Jude, London
Tom Jupp, London

Peter Lavender, Norfolk
Paul Lamb, London
Chris Leigh, London
Gay Lobley, London
Juliet McCaffrey, Brighton
Merron Mitchell, Manchester
Cathy Moorhouse, London
Wendy Moss, London
Anita O'Reilly, Leicester
Julie Northey, Manchester
Mary Osmaston, Manchester
Bob Payne, Norfolk
Roz Pilkington, Manchester
Annie Price, London
John Sanders, Manchester
Sheila Simpson, Manchester
Nancy Steele, Manchester
Jenny Stevens, BBC Development Officer
Alan Tuckett, NIACE
Pauline Walker, Manchester
Jane Ward, Manchester
Jackie Webb, London
Alan Wells, BSA, London
Annie Whiteman, Norfolk
Chris Wild, Leics
Annette Zera, London
NCDS interviewees

References

Abell, S. (1992) *Effective Approaches In Adult Literacy* London: ALBSU

ACACE, (1979) *A Strategy for the Basic Education of Adults* Leicester: ACACE

Ainley, P. and Corney, M. (1990) *Training for the Future: The Rise and Fall of the Manpower Services Commission* London: Cassell

ALBSU (1981) Basic Education and Unemployment *Newsletter* April/May London: ALBSU

ALBSU (1984) *Developments in Adult Literacy and Basic Skills: An Interim Report* London: ALBSU

ALBSU (1985) *Adult Literacy: The First Decade* London: ALBSU

ALBSU (1986) *Annual Report 1985-6* London: ALBSU

ALBSU, (1987) *Annual Report 1986-7* London: ALBSU

ALBSU, (1989) *Progress Profile* London: ALBSU.

ALBSU (1989b) *ESOL: A Nation's Neglect: Research into the Need for English amongst Speakers of Other Languages* London: ALBSU

ALBSU (1991) *Open Learning Centres in England and Wales: Interim report* London: ALBSU

ALBSU (1993) *Open Learning Centres: Final report* London: ALBSU

ALRA (1976) *Adult Literacy: Progress in 1975/6* London: HMSO

ALRA (1977) *Adult Literacy: Developments in 1976/77* London: HMSO

Apple, M. (1982) (ed) *Cultural and Economic Reproduction in education: Essays on Class, Ideology and the State* London: Routledge and Kegan Paul

Apple, M. (1999) Freire, neo-liberalism and education *Discourse: Studies In The Cultural Politics Of Education* 20,1, 5-20

Appleby, Y. and Hamilton, M. (2005) Literacy as Social Practice: Travelling between the Everyday and other Forms of Learning. To appear in Peter Sutherland and Jim Crowther (eds) *Lifelong Learning: Concepts and Contexts*. London: Routledge

Armitage, A., Bryant, B., Dunnil, R., Hammersley, M., Hayes, D., Hudson, A., and Lawes, S. (1999) *Teaching and Training in Post-compulsory Education* Buckingham: Open University Press

Auerbach, E. (1989) The US-UK Initiative Report. *Rapal Bulletin*, Issue 8

Avis, J., Bloomer, M., Esland, G., Gleeson, D. and Hodkinson, P. (eds) (1996) *Education, Politics and Work* London: Cassell

Avis, J., Bathmaker, A-M., and Parsons, J. (2001) Reflections from a time-log diary: towards an analysis of the labour process within further education *Journal of Vocational Education and Training* 53 (1) pp 61-80

Avis, J., Bathmaker, A., and Parsons, J. (2002) Communities of Practice and the Construction of Learners in Post-compulsory Education and Training *Journal of Vocational Educa-*

tion and Training, 54 (1) pp 27 – 50

Ball, S. (1990) *Politics and Policy Making* London: Routledge

Ball, S. (1993) What is Policy? Texts, trajectories and tool boxes *Discourse* 13 (2) pp 10 – 17

Ball, S. (1994) Political Interviews and the politics of interviewing in Walford, pp 96-115

Bandali S. (1976) *Small Accidents: The Autobiography of a Ugandan Asian* Manchester: Gatehouse Books

Banks, H, (1982) 'Adult Basic Education with a group of mentally handicapped and psychiatric residents in Norfolk.' *ALBSU Newsletter* Nov/Dec No.10: pp 6-7 London: ALBSU

Barnes, S. (2005). *Why Gremlins?* St. Luke's Advertising Agency. http://www.dfes.gov.uk/get-on/gremlin.shtml (accessed Nov 2005)

Bartlett, L. and Holland, D. (2002) Theorizing the space of literacy practices *Ways of Knowing* 2 (1) pp 10-22

Barton, D. (1994) *Literacy: An Introduction to the Ecology of Written Language* Oxford: Blackwell

Barton, D. and Hamilton, M. (1998) *Local Literacies: Reading and Writing in One Community* London: Routledge

Barton, D., Hamilton, M. and Ivanic, R. (2000) (eds) *Situated Literacies* London: Routledge

Barton, David, Yvon Appleby, Rachel Hodge, Karin Tusting and Roz Ivanič. (2006) *Relating lives and learning: Adults' Participation and Engagement in a Variety of Settings* London: National Research and Development Centre for Adult Literacy and Numeracy.

Bathmaker. A-M. (2005) Achieving The Basic Skills Targets In England: What Picture Can We Gain From Available Statistical Data And What Issues Does This Raise? Presentation to BERA Conference University of Glamorgan 14-17th Sept 2005

Bayliss, P. (2003) Learning behind bars: time to liberate prison education *Studies in the Education of Adults*, 35:2, pp. 157-172

BBC (undated-) *An Outline of the contribution broadcasting might make to reducing adult illiteracy in the UK* – unattributed discussion paper circulated to LEAs and others in preparation for *On the Move* 197- (in Changing Faces archive)

Benton, L and Noyelle, T. (1992) *Adult Illiteracy and Economic Performance*, OECD Centre for Educational Research and Innovation, Paris

Bergin, S. and Hamilton, M. (1994) Who's at the Centre? The Experience of Open Learning in Adult Basic Education. In Thorpe, M. and Grugeon, D. (eds) *Open Learning in the Mainstream* London: Longman. pp 55-73

Blackfriars Literacy Scheme (1988) Student control or student responsibility *RaPAL Bulletin* (6) Summer 1988

Bloomer, M. (1996) *Curriculum Making in Post-16 education* London: Routledge

Bonnerjea, L. (1987) *Workbase: Trades Union Education and Skills Project: A Research Report* London: ALBSU

Brandt, D. (2005) Writing for a Living: Literacy and the Knowledge Economy *Written Communication* 22 (2) April pp 166-197

Briggs, A., and Burke, P. (2005) *A Social History of the Media: From Gutenberg to the Internet* Cambridge: Polity Press

British Association of Settlements (BAS) (1973) *Status Illiterate, Prospects Zero* London: BAS

British Association of Settlements (1974) *A Right to Read: Action for a Literate Britain* London: BAS

British Association of Settlements (BAS) (1976) *Volunteer Pack* London: BAS

Britten, J. (1975) *The development of writing abilities 11-18* London: London Schools Council

Britten, J., Burgess, T., Martin, N. McLeod, A. and Rosen, H. (1975) *The Development of Writing Abilities (11-18)* London: Macmillan Education

Brooks, G., Giles, K., Harman, J., Kendall. S., Rees, F., and Whittaker, S. (2000) *Assembling the Fragments: A review of research into Adult Basic Skills* London: DfEE

Brooks, G. Davies, R. Duckett, L. Hutchison, D. Kendall, S. and Wilkin, A. (2001) *Assessing Progress in Adult Literacy* BSA

Burnett, J., Vincent, D. and Mayall,D. (eds) (2 vols) (1984 – 1987) *The Autobiography of the Working Class : an annotated, critical bibliography* Brighton : Harvester Press

Burns, T. and Stalker, G. (1961) *The Management of Innovation* London: Tavistock

Bynner, J. and Parsons, S. (1998): *Use it or Lose it?* London: The Basic Skills Agency:

Bynner, J. and Steedman, J. (1995) *Difficulties with Adult Basic Skills.* London: Basic Skills Agency

Bynner,J. and Parsons, S. (1997) *It doesn't get any better: The impact of poor basic skills on the lives of 37 year olds* London: Basic Skills Agency

Cambridge House (1984) *In our Own words: Special Issue of Newsletter* London: Cambridge House Literacy Scheme

Carby, H.V.(1982) Schooling in Babylon *The Empire Strikes Back.* The Centre for Contemporary Cultural Studies London: Hutchinson

Carter, R. and McCarthy, M. (1997) *Exploring Spoken English* Cambridge: CUP

Centerprise (1978) *Centerprise Annual Report* December 1978 London: Centerprise (also reports for years 1982-1986 held in *Changing Faces* archive)

Chappell, C., Farrel, L., Scheeres, H. and Solomon , N. (2000) The organization of identity: Four cases in Symes, C. and McIntyre, J. (eds.) *Working Knowledge: The new vocationalism in higher education* Buckingham: Open University Press

Charnley A. H., and Jones, H. A. (1981) *The Concept of Success in Adult Literacy* London: Adult Literacy and Basic Skills Unit

Charnley, A. H. and Withnall, A. (1989) *Developments in Basic Education: Special Development Projects 1978-85* London: ALBSU

Chitty, C. (2004) *Education Policy in Britain* London: Palgrave.

Chitty, C. (ed) (1990) *Post-16 education: Studies in access and achievement* London: Kogan Page

Chitty, C. (1989) *Onwards a new education system: The Victory of the New Right* London: Falmer Press.

Clarke, J. (1989) *'...This is a lifetime thing': outcomes for Adult Basic Education students from from Hackney Adult Education Institute and the Hackney Reading Centre'.* ALFA (Access to Learning for Adults) London: The North and East London Open College Network.

Clyne, P. (1972) *The Disadvantaged Adult* London: Longman

Coben, D. (2006) The Socio Cultural approach to adult numeracy: issues for policy and practice in Lyn Tett, Mary Hamilton, and Yvonne Hillier (eds) *Adult Language, Literacy and Numeracy: Policy, Practice and Research* Buckingham: Open University Press.

Coben, D. (2003) (ed *Adult Numeracy: A review of research and related literature* London: NRDC

Cockroft, W. (1982) *Mathematics Counts* London: HMSO

Colwell, D. (2003) in Coben, D. (2003) (ed) *Adult Numeracy: A review of research and related literature* London: NRDC

Cox, C.B. and Dyson, A.E. (1969) *Black Paper 2: The Crisis in Education* The Critical Quarterly Society.

Craven, J. and Jackson, F. (1986) *Whose Language? A Teaching Approach for Caribbean Heritage Students* Central Manchester Caribbean English Project Manchester: Manchester Education Committee

Crowther, J., Hamilton, M., and Tett, L. (eds.) (2001) *Powerful Literacies* Leicester: NIACE

Curtis, H. and Sanderson, M. (2004) *The Unsung Sixties: Memoirs of Social Innovation* London: Whiting and Birch

Curzon, L., B., (2004) *Teaching in Further Education: an outline of Principles and Practice 6th edition* London: Continuum

Davies, P. (2000) Formalising Learning: the impact of Accreditation In Coffield, F. (ed) *The Necessity of Informal Learning* Bristol: The Policy Press

Deem, R. (1981) State policy and ideology in the education of women, 1944-1980 *British Journal of Sociology of Education*, 2 (2) pp 131-143

Department for Education and Employment (1999) *Learning to Succeed: A New Framework for Post-16 Learning* White Paper Cmnd 4392. London: DfEE

Department for Education and Employment (1998) *The Learning Age: Renaissance for a New Britain* Green Paper Cmnd 3790 London: The Stationery Office

Department of Education and Science (1973) *Report on Adult Education: a plan for development* (Russell Report) London: HMSO

Department of Education and Science (1975) *A Language for Life: The Bullock Report* London: HMSO

Department for Education and Science (1988) *Report of the Committee of Inquiry into the Teaching of English Language* (The Kingman Report) London: HMSO

Department for Education and Science (1992) *Further and Higher Education Act 1992* London: HMSO

Department for Education and Skills (2001) *Skills for life: The national strategy for improving adult literacy and numeracy skills* London: Department for Education and Skills

Department for Education and Skills (2005) *Get On Campaign – Evaluation Summary* Internal Document, Skills for Life Strategy Unit, April 2005 London: DfES

Devereux, W. (1982) *Adult Education in Inner London 1870-1980* London: ILEA

Drews, W. and Fieldhouse, R. (1996) Residential Colleges and Non-residential Settlements and Centres. in Roger Fieldhouse (ed) *A History of Modern Adult Education* Leicester: NIACE pp 239-263

Dror, Y. (1967) Policy Analysis: a new professional role in government service *Public Administration Review* 27(3) pp 197-203

EDAP Employee Development and Assistance Programme: *Learning Through EDAP: A Joint Initiative by Ford and the Trade Unions* Essex: National EDAP Office.

Eden Grove Women's Group (1982) *Left in the Dark* London: Rathbone Society

Edwards, J (1986) *Working class education in Liverpool: a radical approach* Manchester Monographs: University of Manchester

Ekinsmyth, C. and Bynner, J. (1994) *The Basic Skills of Young Adults* London: Adult Literacy and Basic Skills Unit.

Elmore, R. (1985) Forward and Backward Mapping In Hanf, K. and Toonan,T. (eds) *Policy Implementation in Federal and Unitary Systems* Dordrecht: Martinus Nijhof Publishers

Etzioni, A. (1968) *The Active Society: A Theory of Societal and Political Processes* New York: Free Press

Evans, B. (1992) *The Politics of the Training Market: From MSC to TECs* London: Routledge

Fairclough, N. (2001) The Discourse of New Labour: Critical Discourse Analysis in M. Wetherell, S. Taylor and S. Yates (ed) *Discourse as Data: A Guide for Analysis* Sage. pps 229-266

Fairclough, N. (2003) *Analyzing discourse: Textual analysis for social research* London: Routledge

Fawbert, F. (2003) (ed) *Teaching in Post-compulsory Education: Learning, Skills and Standards* London: Continuum.

FEDA: Further Education Development Agency, now the Learning and Skills Development agency web site: [http://www.lsda.org.uk]. (For access to policy information and downloadable publications)

Feinstein, L. (2003) *The Contribution of Adult learning to Health and Social Capital* London: Centre for Research on the Wider Benefits of Learning, Institute of Education.

Ferri, E., Bynner, J., and Wadsworth, M. (2003) *Changing Britain, Changing Lives: Three Generations at the Turn of the Century* Institute of Education: London.

Further Education National Training Organisation (FENTO) (1999) *Standards for teaching and supporting learning in further education in England and Wales* London: Further Education National Training Organisation.

Further Education Unit (FEU) (1989) *Black Perspectives on Adult Education: Identifying the Needs* London: FEU.

Field, J (1996) Learning for Work: Vocational Education in Roger Fieldhouse (ed) *A History of Modern Adult Education* Leicester: NIACE pp333-353.

Field, J. (2005) *Social Capital and Lifelong Learning* Bristol: The Policy Press

Fieldhouse, R. (ed) (1996) *A History of Modern Adult Education* Leicester: National Institute of Adult Continuing Education

Finch, J. (1984) *Education as Social Policy* London: Longman

Finegold, D., McFarland, L., and Richardson, W. (eds.) (1993) *Something borrowed, something blue? A study of the Thatcher government's appropriation of American education and training policy* Oxfordshire: Triangle Books

Fingeret, A. and Drennon, C. (1997) *Literacy for Life: Adult learners, new practices* London: Teachers College Press

Flanagan, J. (1994) 'Forging a Common Language, Sharing the Power' in Mary Hamilton *et al, Worlds of Literacy* pp 227-236.

Fowler, G. (1988) in Molyneux, F. Low, E. and Fowler, G. *Learning for Life: Politics and Progress in Recurrent Education* London: Croom Helm

Fowler, Z. (2004) Politically constructing adult literacy: A case study of the skills for life strategy for improving adult literacy in England 1997-2002. Institute of Education, University of London Unpublished PhD Thesis (p 17)

Frank, F. (ed) (1992) *Not just a number: Writings by workplace learners* Lancaster: Lancaster University Centre for the Study of Education and Training

Frank, F. and Hamilton, M. (1992) Not Just a Number: Case studies of workplace programmes and employer attitudes in North West England Unpublished final report to the Leverhulme Trust

Frankel, A., Millman, L. and Reeves, F. (eds.) (1998) *Basic Skills and Further Education: Communities confront linguistic elitism and exclusion* Bilston: Bilston College

Freire, P. (1972) *Pedagogy of the Oppressed* Harmondsworth: Penguin Books

Frisch, M. (1998) Oral History and Hard times: a review essay in Robert Perks *The Oral History Reader* London: Routledge, Chapter 3: pp 29-37.

Frost, G., and Hoy, C. (eds) (1980) *Opening Time: A writing resource pack written by students in Basic Education* Manchester: Gatehouse Books

Further Education Funding Council (1998) *Basic Education Subject Area 10 Inspection Report.* Coventry: FEFC

Gardener, S. (1985) *The Long Word Club: The development of written language within adult Fresh Start and Return to Learning programmes* London: ILEA Language and Literacy Unit (now from RaPAL)

Gatehouse Books (1983) *Where do we go from here? Adult Lives without Literacy* Manchester: Gatehouse Books

Gee, J. (2004) *What Video Games Have to Teach Us About Learning and Literacy* Basingstoke: Palgrave Macmillan

Gee, J., Hull, G and Lankshear, C. (1996) *The New Work Order: behind the language of capitalism* London: Allen and Unwin

Glaser, B.G., and Strauss, A. (1967) *The Discovery of Grounded Theory: Strategies for Qualitative Research* London: Weidenfeld and Nicolson

Gleeson, D. and Shane, F. (1999) Managing Ambiguity: between markets and managerialism – a case study *Sociological Review* 47 (3) pp461-490

Goodwin, P. (1998) *Television under the Tories: Broadcasting Policy 1979-1997* London: British Film Institute.

Graff, H. (1987) *The Legacies of Literacy: Continuities and Contradictions in Western Culture and Society* Bloomington: Indiana University Press

Gray, D.E. and Griffin, C. (editors) (2000) *Post-Compulsory Education and the New Millennium* London: Jessica Kingsley Press

Griffin, C. (1987) *Adult Education as Social Policy* London: Croom Helm

Groombridge, J. (1978) *Learning for a Change* Leicester: National Institute for Adult Continuing Education and REPLAN

Hajer, M., and Wagenaar, H. (2003) (eds.) *Deliberative Policy Analysis: Understanding Government in the Network Society* Cambridge: CUP

Halsey, A. H. (1972) *Education and Social Change* (UNESCO). [see http://www.sociology. ox.ac.uk/people/halsey.html]

Hamilton, M. (1996) Adult literacy and basic education. In R. Fieldhouse (Ed.), *A modern history of adult education* Leicester: National Institute for Adult Continuing Education.

Hamilton, M. (1997) Keeping Alive Alternative Visions in Hautecoeur, J. (ed) *ALPHA 97 Literacy and Institutional Environments* Hamburg: UNESCO Institute for Education. (reprinted in Herrington and Kendall, 2005)

Hamilton, M. (2005) Just Do It: Literacies, Everyday Learning and the Irrelevance of Pedagogy Keynote Paper, CRLL International Conference: What Difference a Pedagogy Makes 24 – 25th June 2005 Stirling, Scotland

Hamilton, M., and Stasinopolous, M. (1987) *Literacy, Numeracy and Adults: Evidence from the National Child Development Survey* London: Adult Literacy and Basic Skills Unit

Hamilton, M., Barton, D., and Ivanič, R. (1994) *Worlds of Literacy* Clevedon: Multilingual Matters

Hamilton, M., and Merrifield, J. (1999) Adult Basic Education in the UK: Lessons for the US in *National Centre for the Study of Adult Learning and Literacy Annual Review of Adult Learning and Literacy* San Francisco: Jossey Bass

Hammersley, M., Hayes, D., Hudson, A., and Lawes, S. (1999) *Teaching and Training in Post-compulsory Education* Buckingham: Open University Press

Hargreaves, D. (1980) *Adult literacy and Broadcasting: The BBC's Experience* London: Frances Pinter

Harris, R. and Savitzky, F. (eds) (1988) *My Personal Language History, written by ILEA Further Education and Adult Education Students* London: New Beacon Books

Hartley, P. (1992) The Tip of the Iceberg: State Funding and English Language Provision for Bilingual Adults in the UK: A Critical Review MA Dissertation Lancaster: Department of Educational Research, Lancaster University.

Haviland, R. (1973) *Survey of provision for adult illiteracy in England* Reading: Centre for the Teaching of Reading, Reading University

Herrington, M., and Kendall, A. (2005) *Insights in Research and Practice: A Handbook for Adult Literacy, Numeracy and ESOL Practitioners* Leicester: NIACE

Herrington, M. (1994) Learning at Home: Distance Learning in Adult Basic Education in M. Hamilton *et al Worlds of Literacy* Clevedon: Multilingual Matters pp 182-187

Herrington, M. (2005) Learning about Dyslexia: A longitudinal research and practice case study in professional development in Herrington, M. and Kendall, A. *Insights from Research and Practice: A Handbook for Adult Literacy, numeracy and ESOL Practitioners* Leicester: NIACE (pp615-652).

Hevey, D. (1992) *The Creatures that Time Forgot: Photography and Disability Imagery* London: Routledge.

Hillier, Y. (1991) Introducing Competence Based Courses in Adult Basic Education *Adults Learning* 3 (3) p73

Hillier, Y. (1994) Informal Practitioner Theory in Adult Basic Education Unpublished Doctoral Thesis London: University of East London

Hillier, Y. (1998) Informal Practitioner Theory: Eliciting the Implicit *Studies in the Education of Adults*, 30 (1) pp 35-52

Hillier, Y. (2005) *Reflective Teaching in Adult and Further Education* London: Continuum (2nd edition)

Hillier, Y., and Hamilton, M. (2005) The Changing Face of Adult Literacy, Numeracy and ESOL: from cupboard to classroom CRLL International Conference What Difference a Pedagogy Makes 24 – 25th June 2005 Stirling, Scotland

Hillier, J., and Jameson, J. (2003) *Empowering Researchers in Further Education* Stoke on Trent: Trentham Books

Hillier, Y., and Jameson, J. (2004) *A rich contract? or, the ragged-trousered philanthropy of part-time staff: The deployment and development of part-time staff in the learning and skills sector* London: LSDA

Hodge, R. (2003) *A review of recent ethnographies of literacy* Lancaster: Centre for the study of literacy

Hodgson, A., and Spours, K. (1997) *Dearing and Beyond 14-19 Qualifications, Frameworks and Systems* London: Kogan Page

Hoggart, R. (1957) *The Uses of Literacy: Aspects of working-class life with special reference to publications and entertainment* London: Chatto and Windus

Holland, C. Frank, F. and Cook, T. (1998) *Literacy and the New Work Order* Leicester: NIACE

Holland, D. and Lave, J. (2001) (eds) *History in Person: Enduring struggles, contentious practices, intimate identities* Santa Fe; Oxford: School of American Research Press.

Hoppe, R. (1993) Political judgement and the policy cycle: the case of ethnicity policy arguments in the Netherlands, in Fischer and Forester (eds) *The Argumentative Turn in Policy Analysis and Planning* London: UCL Press

Howard, U. (1991) Self, Education and Writing in Nineteenth-Century English Communities in Barton, D. and Ivanič, R. (eds) *Writing in the Community* London: Sage

Howard, U. (1994) Writing in 19th Century England: Uses and meanings. Unpublished Phd thesis University of Sussex.

Howard, U. (2004) Learning to Write in 19th Century England in *Reflect* Issue 1: NRDC London pp18-20.

Hull, G and Schultz, K (2002) *School's Out! Bridging Out-of-School Literacies with Classroom Practice* New York, Teachers' College Press.

Hull, G., and Schultz, K. (2001) Literacy and learning out of school: a review of theory and practice in *Review of Educational Research.* l 71:4 pp 575-611

Hutchinson, E. (1980) *Freshstart courses* Leicester: NIACE

Hyland, T. and Merrill, B. (2003) *The Changing Face of Further Education: Lifelong Learning, Inclusion and the Community* London: Routledge Falmer

Hyland,T. (1994) *Competence, Education and NVQs: dissenting perspectives* Cassell: London.

ILEA Afro-Caribbean Language and Literacy Project in Further and Adult Education (1990) *Language and Power.* London: Harcourt, Brace Jovanovich.

Ivanic, R. (1998) *The Discoursal Construction of Identity in Academic Writing* Amsterdam: John Benjamins

Jepson, S. (1990) *Contemporary Developments In Adult Basic Education In Greater Manchester* MA Dissertation University of Manchester

Jones, H, and Marriott, S. (1995) Adult Literacy in England 1945-75: Why did it take so long to get On The Move? *History of Education*, 24 (4) pp337-352.

Jones, H. and Charnley, A. (1978) *The Adult Literacy Campaign: A study of its impact* Leicester: NIAE

Jones, K. (2003) *Education in Britain 1944 to the Present* Cambridge: Polity Press

Jones, P.W. (1992) *World Bank financing of education: lending, learning, and development* London, New York : Routledge

Jupp, T and Hodlin, S. (1975) *Industrial English: An example of theory and practice in functional language teaching* London: Heinemann

Kambouri, M., and Francis, H. (1994). *Time to leave? Progression and drop out in basic skills programs* London: Basic Skills Agency

Kambouri, M., Totounji and Francis, H. (1996) *Where Next? Drop-out and progression from ESOL* London: Basic Skills Agency

Kelly, T. (1992) *A History of Adult Education in Great Britain* Liverpool: Liverpool University Press.

Kennedy, H. (1997) *Learning Works: Widening Participation in Further Education* (The Kennedy Report) Coventry: FEFC

Klein, C. and Millar, R. (1993) *Diagnosing Dyslexia* London: Basic Skills Agency

Knowles, M. (1978) *The adult learner: a neglected species* Houston: Gulf Publishing

Kohl, H. (1976) *On Teaching* London: Methuen and Co

Kress, G. (2003) *Literacy and the New Media* London: Routledge

Lankshear, C. and Knobel, M. (2003) *New Literacies: Changing Knowledge and Classroom Learning* Buckingham: Open University Press

Lavender, P., Derrick, J. and Brooks, B. (2004) *Testing, Testing... 123: Assessment in Adult Literacy, language and Numeracy* A NIACE Policy Discussion Paper. Leicester: NIACE.

Law, J. (1994) *Organizing Modernity* Oxford: Blackwell.

Lawes, S. (1999) *Teaching and Training in Post-compulsory Education* Buckingham: Open University Press

Lawrence, J. (1985) *It Used to be Cheating: working together in adult literacy groups* Cambridge: National Extension College

Lawson, J. and Silver, H. (1973) *A Social History of Education in England* London: Methuen.

Levin, B. (2005) Improving research-policy relationships: The case of literacy. In *International Handbook of Educational Policy* pp. 613-628

Limage, L. (1986) Adult Literacy Policy in Industrialised Countries *Comparative Education Review* 30 pp 50-72

Limage, L. (1990) Adult Literacy and Basic Education in Europe and North America: from recognition to Provision *Comparative Education* 26 (1) pp 125-140

Linguistic Minorities Project (1985) *The Other languages of England* London: Routledge and Kegan Paul

Lipsky, M. (1979) *Street Level Bureaucracy* New York: Russell Sage Foundation

Lisbon European Council (2000) *An agenda of Economic and Social Renewal for Europe* http://europa.eu.int/growthandjobs/pdf/lisbon_en.pdf (Accessed Dec 2005)

Lo Bianco, J. (2001) Policy Literacy *Language and Education* 15 (2) pp 212-227

Lo Bianco, J. and Wickert, R. (eds) (2001) *Language and Literacy Policy in Australia: 30 years of Action* Melbourne: Language Australia

Lo Bianco, J., and Freebody, P. (1997) *Australian Literacies: Informing national policy on literacy education* Melbourne: National Languages and Literacy Institute of Australia

Lobley, G. (1989) *The Politics of Literacy: A Study of Adult Literacy in Britain 1975 – 1989* Open University MA

Lobley, G. and Moss, W. (1990) ILEA Goodbye! *RaPAL Bulletin*, Issue 11 Spring.

Lovett, T. (ed) (1988) *Radical Approaches to Adult Education: A Reader* London: Routledge

Lumby, J., and Foskett, NB (2005) *14–19 Education: Policy, Leadership and Learning* London: Sage

Mace, J. (1979) *Working with Words* London: Writers and Readers Publishing Co-operative

Mace, J. (1981) *Something to say... a study in community education*, Lee Centre Adult Reading Scheme London: Goldsmiths' College

Mace, J. (1992) *Talking about Literacy: principles and practice in adult literacy education*, London: Routledge (now forthcoming as an e-book)

Mace, J. (ed.) (1995). *Literacy, Language, and Community Publishing: Essays in adult education*. Clevedon: Multilingual Matters

Mace, J. (1998) Reminiscence as literacy: intersections and creative moments in R. Perks and A. Thomson, eds *The Oral History Reader* London: Routledge.

Mace, J. (2002) Can't someone write a proper test for literacy? *Guardian* (Education) Tuesday May 28th

Mace, J. (2002) *The Give and Take of Writing: Scribes, literacy and everyday life* Leicester: NIACE

Mace, J and Baynham, M. (1986) *Doing Research* Lee Community Education Centre London: Goldsmith's College

Mace, J. and Wendy Moss, W. (1988), *How do People Decide to Join a Literacy Class?* National Federation of Voluntary Literacy Schemes and Lee Community Education Centre.

Mace, J. and Wolfe, M. (1990) Identity, Authorship and Status: Issues for Britain in ILY

Adults Learning 1 (10) pp 267-9

Mace, J. and Yarnit, M. (1987) *Time Off to Learn: Paid educational leave and low-paid workers* London: Methuen

Manpower Services Commission (MSC) (1981) *The Post Training Employment Experience of TOPS Trainees* Sheffield: MSC

Manpower Services Commission (1978) *TOPS Review* Sheffield: MSC

Manpower Services Commission (MSC) (1983) *Towards an Adult Training Strategy A Discussion Paper* April 1983 Sheffield: MSC

Martin, P. (1988) Open College Networks: Success against the odds? *Journal of Further and Higher Education*, 22 (2) pp183-192

Martin-Jones, M. and Jones, K. (2000) *Multilingual Literacies* Amsterdam: John Benjamins

May, J.V. and Wildalvsky, A. (eds) (1978) *The Policy Cycle* Beverley Hills, California: Sage

Mayo, M. (1997) *Imagining Tomorrow: Adult Education for Transformation* Leicester: NIACE

Mayo, M. and Thompson, J. (eds) (1995) *Adult Learning, Critical intelligence and Social Change* Leicester: NIACE

McCulloch, G. and Richardson, W. (2000) *Historical research in Educational Settings* Open University Press

McGivney, V. (2003) (2nd edition) *Staying or Leaving the Course* Leicester: NIACE

McKenna, R. and Fitzpatrick, L. (2004) *Building Sustainable Adult Literacy Provision: A review of international trends in adult literacy policy and programs* Commonwealth of Australia: National Centre for Vocational Education Research (NCVER)

Merry, R. (1984) *More than Reading and Writing: Literacy schemes and other activities* Special Development report to ALBSU. [archived at Ruskin College, Oxford]

Minton, D. (1991) *Teaching Skills in Further and Adult Education* London: City and Guilds/Macmillan

Moore, H. (2002) Who will Guard the Guardians Themselves? National Interest versus Factional Corruption in Policymaking for ESL in Australia in J. Tollefson (ed) *Language Policies in Education* Lawrence Erlbaum

Morley, D and Worpole, K. (eds) (1982) *The Republic of Letters: Working class writing and local publishing* London: Commedia Publishing Group

Morris, C. and Nwenmele, H. (1994) The Kweyol Language and Literacy Project in Hamilton *et al Worlds of Literacy* pp 81-94

Moser, C. (1999) *Improving Literacy and Numeracy: A fresh start The report of the working group chaired by Sir Claus Moser* London: Department for Education and Employment

Moss, W. (1986) *From talk into text : an examination of language experience work in adult basic education* M.A. Dissertation Lancaster University

Moss,W. (1988) *Breaking the Barriers – Eight Case Studies of Women Returning to Learning in North London* ALFA (Access to Learning for Adults) The North and East London Open College Network and REPLAN

Mugglestone, L. (1995) *Talking Proper. The Rise of Accent as a Social Symbol* Oxford: Clarendon Press

Murphy, S. (1990) Den Bosch Days (commentary on an International Literacy Year Conference in Holland) *RaPAL Bulletin* Issue 13 – Autumn

National Research and Development Centre for Literacy, Numeracy and ESOL (NRDC) www.nrdc.org.uk

Newman, J. (1994) Gender and Politics of change, in Clarke, J, A. Cochrane and E.

McLaughlin (eds) *Managing Social Policy* London: Sage

Newman, J. (2001) *Modernising Governance* London: Sage

Norris, M. (1984) *Wood Words and Numbers: A report on a linked Skills Course at the Lee Community Educatin Centre.* Problems of Representation Series London: Lee Centre, School of Adult and Community Studies, Goldsmiths' College

O'Rourke, R. and Mace, J. (1992) *Versions and Variety: Student Publishing in Adult Literacy Education* London: Goldsmiths College

O'Rourke, R. (2005) *Creative Writing: Education, Culture and Community* Leicester: NIACE

O'Rourke, R., Pearse, J., and Tinman, A. (1992) Wordpower and the Publishing of Student Writing. Research and Practice in Adult Literacy *RaPAL Bulletin* Issue 19

Organization for Economic Cooperation and Development/Centre for Educational Research and Innovation (OECD/CERI) (1973) *Recurrent Education: A Strategy for Lifelong learning* OEDC: Paris

Organization for Economic Cooperation and Development (OECD/Stats Canada) (1995) *Literacy, Economy and Society: Results of the First International Adult Literacy Survey* Paris: OECD

Organization for Economic Cooperation and Development (OECD) (1997) *Literacy skills for the knowledge society* Paris: OECD

Organization for Economic Cooperation and Development. (OECD) (2000) *Literacy in the Information Age: Final Report of the International Adult Literacy Survey* Paris: OECD

Organization for Economic Cooperation and Development/Centre for Educational Research and Innovation (OECD/CERI)(1997) *Education Policy Analysis 1997* Paris: OECD

Ozga, J. (1993) *Women in Educational Management* Buckingham: Open University Press.

Ozga, J. (2000) *Policy Research in Educational Settings: Contested Terrain* Buckingham: Open University Press

Parkes, D. (1985) Competition ... and Competence? Education, training and the role of the DES and MSC in Ian McNay and Jenny Ozga (eds) *Policy Making in Education* Buckingham: Pergamon Press with the Open University pp 159-172.

Parsons, S., and Bynner, J. (1999) *Literacy, Leaving School and Jobs: the effect of poor basic skills on employment in different age groups* London:The Basic Skills Agency

Parsons, W. (1995) *Public Policy: An Introduction to the theory and practice of policy analysis* Aldershot: Edward Elgar

Pecket Well College (1989) *As We See Ourselves: Weekend Residential Course Report* Halifax: Pecket Well College

Percy K. and Ward, P. (1991) *The progress of unemployed adults in three Open Colleges Final report of FEU REPLAN Project RP 464* London: FEU

Perks, E; and Thomson, A. (eds) (1998) *The Oral History Reader* London: Routledge

Plowden Report: Central Advisory Council for Education (England) (1967) *Children and their Primary Schools* London: HMSO

Popular Memory Group (1998) Popular memory theory, politics, method in E. Perks and A. Thomson *The Oral History Reader* London: Routledge pp 75-86

Preston, R. (2004) Cultures of funding, management and learning in the global mainstream International *Journal of Educational Development* 25 (2) pp157-172

Raffe, D. (1997) *The Unification of Post-Compulsory Education: Towards a Conceptual Framework* Edinburgh: Centre for the Study of Educational Sociology

RaPAL (2001) *Consultation: social Security Regulations 2001* at www.literacy.lancs.ac.uk/rapal/archive/policy accessed Dec 2005

Reder, S. (in press) Giving Literacy Away, Again: New Concepts of Promising Practice in A. Belzer and H. Beder (eds) *Toward defining and improving quality in adult basic education: Issues and Challenges* New Jersey: Erlbaum.

Rittel, H., and Webber, M. (1973) Dilemmas in a general theory of planning *Policy Sciences* 4 pp155-159

Roberts, C., Davies, E. and Jupp, T. (1992) *Language and discrimination: a study of communication in multi-ethnic workplaces* London: Longman

Robinson, J. (1983) Broadcasting and Adult Learning in UK 1922-1982 in Tight, M. *Education for Adults* Oxford University Press

Rogers, B. (1984) The Trend of Reading Standards Reassessed *Educational Research* Vol. 26 (3) pp153-166

Rogers, J., (1989) *Teaching Adults* (3rd edition) Buckingham: Open University Press

Rosen. C., and Rosen, H. (1973) *The Language of Primary School Children* Harmondsworth: Penguin

Sanders, J. (undated) *Students Said... a Report on the experiences of 48 adult literacy students* Manchester Adult Literacy Research Project.

Sanguinetti, G. (1999) Within and Against Performativity: Discursive Engagement in Adult Literacy and Basic Education. Unpublished PhD. Deakin University, Australia. Chapter 6: A Window on Discursive Engagement pp137-173

Sargant, N. (1992) *Adult Learners, Broadcasting and Channel 4* London: Channel 4

Sargant, N. (1993) *Basic Skills at Work Pilot* London: ALBSU

Sargant, N. (2000) *The Learning Divide Revisited* Leicester: NIACE

Sargant, N., and Aldridge, F. (2003) *Adult learning and social division – a persistent pattern: a report of the findings of a UK-wide survey on adult participation in education and learning* Leicester : National Institute of Adult Continuing Education pp 134-135

Sargant, N. and Tuckett, A. (1997) *Pandora's Box: Companion Papers on Motivation, Access and the Media* Leicester: National Institute of Adult Continuing Education

Schellekens, P. (2001) *English Language as a Barrier To Employment, Education And Training* London: Department for Education and Employment

Schools Council (1967) *Project in English for Immigrant Children (SCOPE)* Leeds: Schools Council, Leeds University

Schuller, T., Hammond, C., Bassett-Grundy, A., Preston, J. and Bynner, J. (2004) *The Benefits of Learning: The Impact of Education on Health, Family Life and Social Capital* London: Routledge

Schwab, I. Stone, J (1987) *Language, writing and publishing Afro-Caribbean Language and Literacy Project* London: Inner London Education Authority

Scribner, S. (1984) Literacy in three metaphors *American Journal of Education* 93 p21

Scribner, S., and Cole, M. (1981) *The Psychology of Literacy* Cambridge, MA: Harvard University Press

Searle, C. (1971) *Stepney Words* (self published)

Searle, C. (1982) Five Girls: Classroom Interaction and Informal Speech In *Becoming our own Experts* The Vauxhall Papers London: ILEA English Centre

Shahnaz, I., and Hamilton, M. (2005) in Herrington and Kendall (eds) *Insights in Research and Practice: A Handbook for Adult Literacy, Numeracy and ESOL Practitioners* Leicester: NIACE

Sharp, R, Green, A and Lewis, J. (1975) *Education and Social Control: a study on progressive primary education* London: Routledge and Kegan Paul

Shrapnel-Gardener, S (1984) *Conversations with Strangers* Teaching Pack and Report of an ALBSU Writing Development Project London: Adult Literacy and Basic Skills Unit

Schwab, I. and Stone, J (1987) *Language, Writing and Publishing Afro-Caribbean Language and Literacy Project* London: Inner London Education Authority

Simon, B. (1988) (ed) *The Search for Enlightenment: Adult Education and the Working Class* London: Lawrence and Wishart Ltd

Simon, B and Chitty, C. (1993) (eds) *Education Answers Back: critical responses to government policy* London: Lawrence and Wishart

Simon, H. (1957) *Models of Man: Social and Rational* New York: John Wiley

Smith, D. (1977) *Racial Disadvantage in Britain: The PEP report*

Smith F., and Miller, G.A.(1966) *The Genesis of Language: a psycholinguistic approach* Massachusetts: MIT Press

Soler, J. and Openshaw, R. (2005) *Literacy Crises and Reading Policies: Children Still can't read!* Routledge

Start, K.B. and Wells, B.K. (1972) *The Trend of Reading Standards* Windsor, Berks; National Foundation for Educational Research.

Stephens, W.B. (1990) Literacy in England, Scotland and Wales, 1500-1900 in *History of Education Quarterly* 30 (4) Special Issue on History of Literacy pp 545-571.

Strauss, A.and Corbyn, J.M. (1990) *Basics of Qualitative Research: Grounded theory Procedures and Techniques* London: Sage

Street, B. (1993) (ed) *Cross-cultural Approaches to Literacy* Cambridge: Cambridge University Press

Street, B. (2004) (ed) *Literacies across Educational contexts: Mediating Learning and Teaching* Caslon

Students at the Adult Literacy Classes at Brighton Polytechnic (1978) *Words in Focus: A book of writing, conversations, and photographs* Brighton: Brighton Polytechnic

Students of Blackfriars Settlement Literacy Scheme (undated) *Yours and Ours* London: Blackfriars Settlement

Tett, L, Hamilton, M, Hillier, Y. (2006) *Adult Literacy, Numeracy and Language: Policy, Practice and Research* Milton Keynes: OUP

Thompson, J. (1983) *Learning liberation : women's response to men's education* London: Croom Helm

Tomlinson, K. (1992) More Ripples in the European Pond (students and tutors making European links) *RaPAL Bulletin* Issue 19 – Autumn

Tomlinson, K. (1994) Growing into Europe: A Report of a Writing Weekend in Belgium 1993 *RaPAL Bulletin* Issue 23 – Spring

Tomlinson, J. (1996) *Inclusive Learning: Report of the Learning Difficulties and/or Disabilities Committee* chaired by Professor John Tomlinson Coventry: Further Education Funding Council

Tomlinson, M. (2004) 14-19 *Curriculum and Qualifications Reform* Final Report of the Working Group on 14-19 Reform Annesley: DfES

Trades Union Congress (TUC) www.tuc.org.uk [accessed Dec 2005]

UNESCO (1997) CONFINTEA *Adult Education, The Hamburg Declaration: The Agenda for the Future* Fifth International Conference on Adult Education 14-18 July 1997 Paris: UNESCO

UNESCO (2006) *Literacy for Life: Global monitoring Report* London and Paris: UNESCO/DfiD

UNESCO (1997) *Literacy and Lifelong Learning* Washington DC: National Institute for Literacy

Vincent, D. (1981) *Bread, Knowledge and Freedom: a study of nineteenth-century working class autobiography* London: Europa

Vincent, D. (2000) *The Rise of Mass Literacy: reading and writing in modern Europe* Malden, MA: Polity Press

Walford, G. (ed) (1994) *Researching the Powerful in Education* London: UCL

Wallis, J. and Elsey, B. (1981) Student Performance and Experiences on TOPS Clerical Training Courses: Parts One and Two *The Vocational Aspect of Education* 23(84) pp 5-11 and (85) pp 31-38

Warnock Report Committee of Enquiry into the Education of Handicapped Children and Young People (1978) *Special Educational Needs: Report of the Committee of Enquiry* Cmnd 7212 London: HMSO

Westwood, S., and Thomas, J.E. (eds) (1991) *The Politics of Adult Education* Leicester: NIACE

White, A. (1963) *The Story of Army Education 1643-1963* London: Harrap

Whitty, T. (1993) Pieces of Paper: A Survey of Student Attitudes towards Accreditation in Adult Literacy and English Classes in Southwark in *RaPAL Bulletin*, Issue 21

Williams, R. (1965) *The Long Revolution* London: Penguin

Withnall, A. (1994) Literacy on the agenda: The origins of the adult literacy campaign in the United Kingdom *Studies in the Education of Adults* 26(1) pp67-85

Wodak, R. (2001) The Discourse-Historical Approach in Wodak, R. and Meyer, M. (eds) *Methods of Critical Discourse Analysis* London: Sage pp 63-94

Wodak, R. and Meyer, M. (2001) *Methods of Critical Discourse Analysis* London: Sage

Wolf, A. (2002) *Does Education Matter? Myths about Education and Economic Growth* Harmondsworth: Penguin.

Workplace Basic Skills Network www.lancs.ac.uk/wbsnet [accessed Dec 2005]

Yarnit M. (1980) Second Chance to Learn, Liverpool: Class and Adult Education in Jane Thompson (ed) 1980 *Adult Education for a Change* London: Hutchinson

Yeatman, A. (ed) (1998) *Activism and the Policy Process* London: Allen and Unwin

Index